# Sports Science
# for Young People

## by George Barr

*Illustrated by*
*Mildred Waltrip*

Dover Publications, Inc., New York '90

Published in Canada by General Publishing Company, Ltd., 30 Lesmill
Road, Don Mills, Toronto, Ontario.
Published in the United Kingdom by Constable and Company, Ltd.,
3 The Lanchesters, 162–164 Fulham Palace Road, London W6 9ER.

This Dover edition, first published in 1990, is an unabridged and
unaltered republication of the work originally published in 1962 under the
title *Young Scientist and Sports* by Whittlesey House, McGraw-Hill Book
Company, Inc., New York.

Manufactured in the United States of America
Dover Publications, Inc., 31 East 2nd Street, Mineola, N.Y. 11501

*Library of Congress Cataloging-in-Publication Data*

Barr, George, 1907–
    [Young scientist and sports]
    Sports science for young people / by George Barr.
        p.      cm.
    Reprint. Originally published: Young scientist and sports. New York :
McGraw-Hill, 1962.
    Includes index.
    Summary: Explains how scientific principles affect the way athletes
perform, particularly in football, basketball, and baseball.
    ISBN 0-486-26527-7
    1. Sports—Juvenile literature. 2. Science—Juvenile literature.
3. Physics—Juvenile literature. [1. Sports. 2. Science. 3. Physics.]
I. Title.
GV706.8.B37    1990
796—dc20                                                    90-40765
                                                               CIP
                                                               AC

# Contents

# Introduction

It is always great fun to play in or watch a baseball, football, or basketball game. But you can double your pleasure in these and other sports by looking at them with the understanding that science brings.

This book directs your attention to many scientific principles underlying modern sports. You will learn how an athlete is able to improve his technique by letting science work *for* him instead of *against* him. You will observe certain actions of experts which you may have overlooked before, and these may help you become a better player yourself. Then you too will be able to save split-seconds and gain inches and accuracy when you play. All good players—and especially champions —use scientific techniques, whether they are aware of them or not.

In the following chapters you will find answers to hundreds of science questions you may have been wondering about. For example, do you know why most fast baseball pitchers are tall men? Does a baseball really curve? Why does a bat sometimes sting or break? How does an electronic, automatic umpire work?

In football, why does a lineman crouch? Why is a football made to spiral when it is passed? In blocking, why is an upward motion used in addition to a forward push?

How is the bounce of a basketball tested before a game? Why do basketball shoes behave like "4-wheel brakes"?

And no science book on sports would be complete without a chapter about the athlete's body. What is a Charley horse? How are black and blue marks caused? Is there such a thing as an "athlete's heart"? How often does a sprinter breathe during a 100-yard dash? What is a "tennis arm"? What actually happens during a knockout?

The most attention in this book has been given to baseball, football, and basketball. However, an additional chapter on other sports is included to illustrate principles you will observe while you are engaged in or watching these sports. For example, do you know why a golf ball has dimples? Why you can't ice skate on glass? How you keep your balance on a bike?

All in all—this very special book is your science companion on the baseball diamond, the basketball court, the football field, or anywhere that exciting events in the world of sports are occurring.

## Sports and motion

When we speak about sports we are referring to games or contests involving force and motion. It is difficult to describe a baseball, basketball, or football game without using many action words. Nor can we omit these words when telling about tennis, golf, track events, swimming, and dozens of other sports.

There is pleasure in seeing a great athlete perform. As we watch his perfect coordination we are aware that it takes many years to reach such a state of perfection. We know that he has had constant exercises in physical strength, speed, and skill. We also know that he has had to study his own body, to improve his strong points, and to eliminate his weaknesses.

But, in addition to this, a good athlete has to know the scientific principles involved in motion. He has to learn to use them to full advantage whenever the opportunities arise. By careful study and planning he can shave seconds or get that extra push champions need in order to break records.

If you too are aware of this strategy, and also of the forces involved in motion, you will get greater enjoyment from any sport you engage in or watch.

Let us review some basic ideas about motion, because we shall refer to them constantly in every sport.

## Things start moving slowly

You are probably already aware of this important fact about motion. You know that automobiles must start slowly. On your TV screen you have seen how slowly huge rockets always leave their launching sites before they gather speed.

About 300 years ago Sir Isaac Newton, an English scientist, formulated many laws about motion. One of them states: *An object at rest tends to remain at rest unless some force causes a change.*

A force, as used by a scientist, is either a push or a pull. In other words, an object which is not moving will remain that way *forever* unless it is moved by muscles, gravity, wind, explosions, electricity, or other force.

When a force starts to be exerted, the object starts moving *slowly* at first. This is because the object resists being moved. This tendency to stay in the same place, is called INERTIA (in-ER-shuh). It is a resistance to change. You will read a great deal in this book about inertia of objects at rest. Many actions in sports can be explained with this law of motion.

For example:
1. At a track meet, a sprinter starts slowly as he overcomes inertia.
2. A baseball player at bat must be well into his swing when the pitcher's fast ball reaches him. It takes time to overcome the inertia of his bat and his muscles.

3. When a swimmer makes a high dive into the water at a wrong angle, he may hurt himself, because of the inertia of the water.

## Inertia of moving objects

Another part of Newton's law of inertia states: *An object in motion tends to continue in motion, at the same speed and in the same direction, unless some force causes a change.*

Were you ever in a moving automobile when the brakes were applied suddenly? Did you find that your body continued to move forward as the car slowed down? And when the car made a sharp right turn, did you sway to the left? That was because you continued to go straight ahead in space as the car made the right turn.

The tendency of moving objects to continue moving in the same direction is also inertia. You have learned about inertia of objects at rest. Now you know that there can also be inertia of moving things.

Inertia then, is the tendency of moving objects and stationary objects to continue what they are doing. For example, we say that the inertia of the earth and other planets keeps them moving.

In sports the players, balls, bats, golf clubs, or tennis rackets usually move very fast. It often takes a great deal of force to stop or change their direction of motion. Inertia plays a big part in influencing the games.

Here are some examples of the inertia of moving objects:

1. A baseball player, sprinting to first base, cannot stop

at the base because of his inertia. The rules allow him to run past it without being tagged out—provided he touches the base as he passes.

2. A batter sometimes swings at an unwanted pitched ball. He cannot stop in time because of the inertia of his muscles and also the inertia of the moving bat. Should he miss the ball, inertia may even swing him around completely.

3. A football player running with the ball will suddenly change direction. He does this to escape the pursuing tackler. The inertia of the tackler makes him continue for an instant in the same direction he was moving.

## Duration of a force affects motion

It is obvious that the longer a force acts on an object to speed it up, the faster it will move. Suppose a player is preparing to throw a ball. At the instant that he starts his swing with his arm behind him, the ball is moving very slowly.

As he overcomes inertia, the ball in his hand moves faster and faster. The longer he holds the ball before he releases it, the faster it moves.

In golf and tennis, good players always continue their swings as long as possible. Baseball batters also take long swings. This is called FOLLOWING-THROUGH. It makes the force act longer on the ball to make it go faster.

At a track meet, you can see how the hammer thrower swings around several times before he lets go. In the javelin throw, the athlete holds on as long as possible

Time between each position of ball shown is 1/100th of a second

by making a complete about-face before hurling the pole.

This same principle is used in reverse when a force *slows down* an object. When a baseball player catches a fast ball he draws the glove to him. This technique increases the time that the *slowing-down force* of his glove is acting. Therefore, the ball does not strike the glove with too strong an impact. This lessens the danger of the ball bouncing out of the glove. It also offers less "sting."

For the same reason, when a football player catches the ball, his body "gives" with the ball. This extra fraction of a second is sufficient to slow down the speed of the ball.

## Speed, weight, and impact

The faster a football player runs, the greater will be his impact as he strikes an opposing player. It is also a well-known fact that the heavier the player, the greater will be his impact at the same speed.

A light weight, such as a bullet, can have much hitting force when it is going fast. On the other hand, a heavy weight, such as a truck, can cause the same impact if it is going slowly.

These effects are due to MOMENTUM (moh-MENT-um). Stated simply, a moving object's momentum is calculated by multiplying its speed by its weight. A 200-pound player moving at 3 miles an hour has as much momentum, or striking force, as a 100-pound player moving at 6 miles per hour.

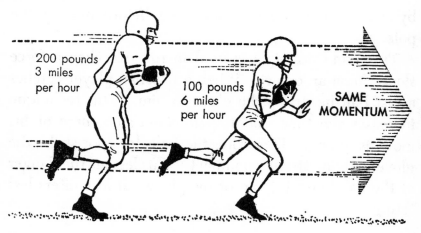

200 pounds
3 miles
per hour

100 pounds
6 miles
per hour

SAME
MOMENTUM

This is one of the reasons why heavy men are selected to be football players. Of course, it is more difficult for a heavy player to get into motion. But once he starts moving, it requires more force to stop him.

In baseball, the weight of the ball cannot be changed. However, the speed of the ball can be increased by faster pitching or harder hitting. The result is that the ball moves with more momentum. Such balls travel far. They also strike the players' gloves with resounding impacts.

## Action and reaction

Another very important law of motion can help explain many activities in sports. It states: *Every action force has an equal and opposite reaction force.*

Strange as it may seem to you, whenever you exert any force upon an object, the object exerts a similar force upon you—but in an opposite direction!

When you kick a football with a certain force, the football pushes your foot right back with the same force. When a bat strikes a baseball, the ball exerts an equal but opposite force upon the bat. And when a basketball hits the backboard, the backboard pushes the ball back with the same force that it was struck.

Two objects are always involved in reaction. One body can never exert a force upon another one without the second reacting against the first. The reacting force is always equal, but in an opposite direction.

How do we walk or run? This may sound silly, but you go forward because you push backward against the

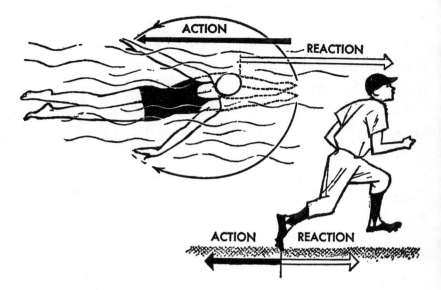

ground. You can convince yourself of this. Try to run on ice. Because of the lack of friction, there will be little *action* against the ground. Therefore, there will be very little *reaction* pushing you forward.

Spiked shoes, cleats, and rubber sneakers are worn by athletes in order to increase friction and get better reaction.

A sprinter at the starting line digs his feet into holes in the track. This enables him to exert more backward force against the ground when the gun is shot. The ground can now push him forward quickly. Sometimes a steel supporting frame is used at the starting line instead of the holes.

A swimmer, too, goes forward because of reaction. The resistance of the water enables the swimmer's hands and feet to exert a backward force. The reaction to this causes the forward motion of the swimmer.

16

# The pull of gravity

The invisible force which pulls everything to the center of the earth is called GRAVITY.

When a ball is tossed high into the air, it moves against this force. That is why the ball loses motion until it finally stops. Then, as gravity pulls the ball down, it gathers more and more speed until it strikes the earth.

Scientists have calculated that it takes just as long for a ball to come down as it took the ball to reach its peak on the way up. They can also prove that the ball strikes the earth with the same speed that it left the hand.

Every person is constantly working against gravity just by moving his own body weight from place to place. High jumpers, pole vaulters, shot-putters, discus and hammer throwers are very much aware of this pulling force!

# A ball takes a curved path

When a ball is thrown or batted upward or horizontally, it always takes a curved path. That is because the earth attracts the ball at an even rate the instant it goes into the air.

All falling objects, regardless of weight or size, fall 16 feet in one second, 64 feet in two seconds, 144 feet in three seconds, and 256 feet in four seconds. It makes no difference whether the objects are dropped or thrown.

The curved path taken by balls, bullets, or other projectiles is called a TRAJECTORY (truh-JECT-ory). Players have learned from experience where a certain trajectory

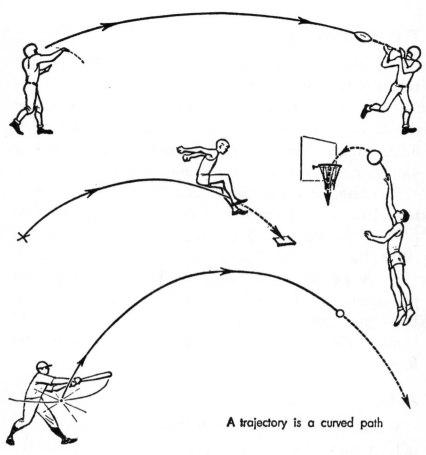

A trajectory is a curved path

will land a ball. That is how a fielder knows exactly where to "get under" a fly ball. Batters learn to estimate the trajectories of the pitched balls. A catcher uses the proper low trajectory when a player attempts to steal second base. The second baseman can now tag the runner with little loss of time or motion.

Football passes, basketball goal shots, and even running-broad jumps are just a few examples of the importance of obtaining the proper trajectory.

# BASEBALL

## Baseball pitching

The pitcher is one of the most important players on the baseball team. Upon him usually depends the success or loss of a game. Because of the sensitive nature of his work all his teammates pamper him. They try in every way to save his strength and his nervous system.

A pitcher must have intelligence, strength, and poise. He is a marvel of coordination. He has trained his eyes and the muscles of his fingers, wrists, arms, legs, back, and hips. His brain tells him the precise moment when his hand must release the ball to deliver a strike. So important is the well-being of a pitcher that he can be "off his game" if he has anything wrong with him. A little ache or pain or some nervousness may prevent him from doing his best.

On the average, only 100 to 150 pitches are made by one pitcher in a game. But every throw is carefully planned and executed. Pitching is hard work and the pitcher is rarely asked to work for the next few days.

See how he saves his energy while he is on the mound. When a catcher wishes to talk to him, he comes up to the pitcher. The pitcher does not walk around too much or make unnecessary motions. He rests between throws.

And the throws are never made too quickly, one after the other.

He may relieve tension by chewing gum. He tries not to be bothered by the jeers or heckling of the spectators. He needs a calm and even disposition, especially when he gets into tight spots.

Notice how he protects his pitching hand by receiving balls from the catcher with his gloved hand only. He also tries not to use his pitching hand when catching a very fast batted ball.

Before a relief pitcher comes in, he warms up in the "bull-pen." [After he warms up he wears his jacket to avoid a chill, which might tighten up his muscles.] When such a pitcher comes to the mound he is allowed up to eight trial pitches to loosen his muscles, and prevent a "glass arm."

Can you observe other ways in which a pitcher is treated like a rare piece of china?

## The strike zone

In order for a strike to be called, the pitcher must deliver a ball in the space over home plate. It must also be between the batter's armpits and the tops of his knees.

The part of home plate facing the pitcher is 17 inches wide. The distance between the knees and armpits varies, of course, for short and tall players. Also, some players crouch and others stand more erect. For a semi-erect stance, the average distance between the top and bottom limits of the strike zone is about 36 to 39 inches.

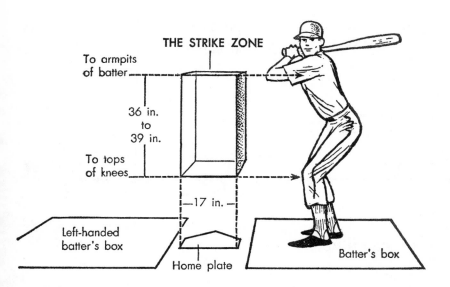

THE STRIKE ZONE

To armpits of batter

36 in. to 39 in.

To tops of knees

—17 in. —

Left-handed batter's box

Home plate

Batter's box

The pitcher makes no attempt to throw every ball in the center of the strike zone. He tries to confuse the batter. He temptingly throws an assortment of high, low, inside, and outside pitches in the strike zone. He also tries to have batters swing at pitches outside the strike zone. A good pitcher knows the weaknesses of every batter on opposing teams.

## The pitcher's mound

The pitcher stands on a little hill or mound. At every pitch he must rest one foot against a rectangular slab of rubber 24 inches long and 6 inches wide. The nearest edge of this pitcher's plate is 60 feet, 6 inches from home base.

The trajectory of any pitched ball is lowered considerably over that distance. The pitcher's mound is therefore raised 15 inches about the level of the base lines.

But even with this aid, a pitcher still has to throw every ball slightly upward. You can see this if you follow a pitched ball carefully.

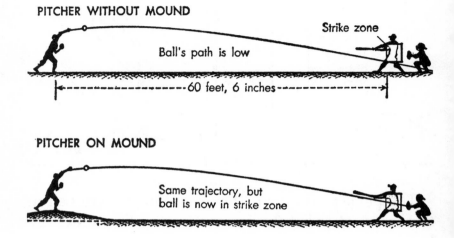

PITCHER WITHOUT MOUND

Strike zone

Ball's path is low

60 feet, 6 inches

PITCHER ON MOUND

Same trajectory, but ball is now in strike zone

The distance between batter and pitcher has been designed to make a more even match between these two players. For the first fifty years of baseball, the pitcher stood 55 feet from home plate. In 1893, this distance was increased to 60 feet, 6 inches. It is good to keep in mind that the distances, apparatus, and rules used in baseball have been changed many times. Each change has made the game more competitive and thrilling to watch.

Some sports writers and commentators refer to the mound as the pitcher's "box." The reason is that before 1900 the pitcher actually had to stand in a white lined area called a BOX. So you see, some expressions never die!

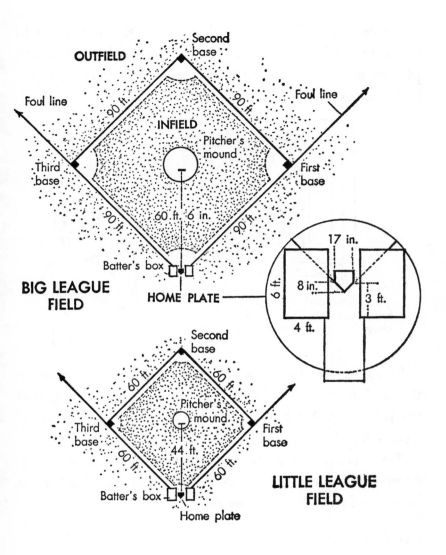

The mound is a circle cleared of grass, usually 15 to 18 feet in diameter. An interesting experiment to check this measurement is the following:

Hold a pencil or a stick vertically at arm's length.

Sight past this object toward the pitcher when he is in the center of the mound. Compare the height of the pitcher and the diameter of the mound by making reference marks on the pencil.

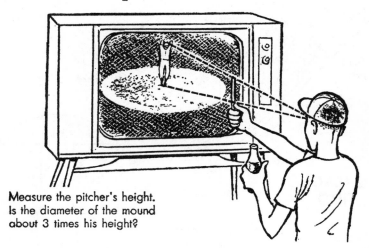

Measure the pitcher's height. Is the diameter of the mound about 3 times his height?

Suppose you find that the mound diameter is about three times the height of the pitcher. Assuming that the pitcher is about 6 feet tall, the diameter of the mound would be 18 feet.

Try this next time you see a professional game on TV, or at a stadium. You will find that not all ball parks have similar pitchers' mounds.

## Little-League pitcher's mound

This little hill is 8 feet in diameter and rises gradually to a peak which is 6 inches above the level of home plate. The official distance between the nearest edge of home plate and the nearest edge of the pitcher's plate is 44 feet.

# The pitcher's windup

Many people believe that the long windmill type of windup is mainly for the purpose of confusing the batter. Some pitchers however, have developed a style which does not include an elaborate windup. Most experts believe that when the windup is done correctly, it limbers up the pitcher's muscles. It also gives the ball the most snap when it leaves the pitcher's hand.

There are several very good scientific reasons for the long stretch and fast motions of the windup. In order to get the most speed into a pitched ball, the pitcher must increase speed as long as possible before the ball leaves his hand.

The pitcher does this by holding the ball as far back as he can. He gets back still farther by lifting one leg off the ground and bending the knee of the other leg. This motion also lowers his entire body.

When he comes forward, his feet act as the center of a large circle for which his legs, body, and arm act as the radius. The ball can now move in as large an arc as possible. As he continues forward, and his body is thrown off balance, he takes a stride forward. Every split-second, the force of the pitcher's muscles keeps speeding up the ball more and more. (See illustration on page 13.) When his throwing arm is as far forward as he can get it, the pitcher releases his fingers. The inertia of the moving ball makes it continue to home plate.

If the pitcher releases the ball too early, it is high; if too late, the ball is low.

The explosive snap of the pitcher's wrist, legs, and trunk also gives the body an extra burst of speed. If you watch carefully, you will see how he pushes back against the rubber plate with his foot. This is done just as he releases the ball. The reaction of the plate gives his body an extra shove forward. The momentum of the body at the finish is so great, that generally the back foot is dragged several inches along the ground.

Every pitcher uses a different kind of windup—whichever he has found successful. And after every delivery, there is his follow-up. This places him in a position to field a ball hit to him.

Notice that the pitcher comes down flat-footed. If he came down on his heel, it would jar him and he would lose control slightly.

It is also interesting to note that tall pitchers specialize in throwing very fast balls. The extra height enables them to make the ball go through a longer arc during the windup. The ball now has a longer time to be speeded up before delivery.

## Kinds of pitches

When baseball was first introduced as a sport, the batter had the privilege of telling the pitcher just where he wanted him to pitch. He asked for a low or a high ball.

Today, of course, the pitcher tries to fool the batter with a variety of pitches. Most pitchers use mainly:
1. The fast ball.
2. The curve ball.

3. The change-of-pace ball, also called CHANGE-UP. This pitch approaches the plate slowly. It can be a half-speed fast ball or a slow curve. It confuses the batter and makes him change his timing.

In addition, there are special pitches which are really variations of a curve ball. They are not used as often as the three listed above because they are difficult to perfect and to control. These include: knuckle ball, screwball, slider, fork ball and several others.

## Does a ball really curve?

There have been many arguments as to whether a ball actually curves or whether this is only an optical illusion. For over fifty years, all kinds of testing apparatus have been devised by eager laymen and scientists in order to find the truth. Photography, flashing lights, wind tunnels, and tapes attached to balls have been used.

Pitched curve balls have been thrown parallel to vertical posts lined up in a straight line. Measurements were taken of the distance of the ball from each post as it shot by. It was found that the path of the ball did indeed curve.

The most recent convincing research was done by Dr. Lyman Briggs, former head of the National Bureau of Standards. He attached a long strip of fine flat tape to a baseball. He then had a good pitcher throw a curve the regulation distance. He counted the number of twists in the tape. This told him how many complete spins the ball made in 60 feet, 6 inches. Then he set up a baseball in a wind tunnel used in aeronautics research.

He spun the ball at the rate determined by his experiments with the twisted tape.

Dr. Briggs concluded that it is possible for a pitcher to make the ball curve. The bend can be as much as 17½ inches from a straight line between home plate and the pitcher's mound. This "ideal curve" travels about 100 feet per second. The ball has to be spun around an axis at 1,800 revolutions per minute.

## Why does a ball curve?

A pitcher makes the ball curve by giving the wrist a hard snap as he releases the ball. The ball comes off the side of his index finger and his thumb. Aided by the friction of the fingers against the seams, the ball is set spinning on its axis.

POSITION FOR THROWING A CURVE

Look at the diagram of the spinning ball moving through the air. Its axis is vertical.

As the ball spins, there is friction against the air close to it. This causes some of the air to be dragged around by the spinning ball.

As the ball goes forward, it meets oncoming air which acts like a wind. On the left side of the ball, there is increased air resistance as the air carried by the ball

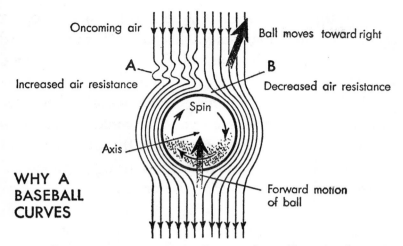

Oncoming air

Ball moves toward right

A

B

Increased air resistance

Decreased air resistance

Spin

Axis

WHY A
BASEBALL
CURVES

Forward motion
of ball

meets the air coming *toward* it. This piles up the air at A.

On the right side of the ball, the air that is carried by the ball now travels *with* the oncoming air. This makes the air resistance less at B. The ball follows the path of least resistance and moves toward the right. As it keeps doing this along the entire flight, a curved path is the result.

There is another way of explaining curves. Notice that at B, the air speed is increased, because the oncoming air and the air around the spinning ball are spinning *together*.

It is a well-known scientific fact that when air is made to move faster, its pressure gets less. Therefore, the air pressure at B is less than at A.

Throughout the flight of the spinning baseball, the higher air pressure on the left pushes the ball toward the lower air pressure on the right.

The ball in the diagram will produce a curve which

turns *toward* a right-handed batter. It is called an INSIDE curve. In baseball language, this curve "breaks" toward the batter. It is the natural curve of a left-handed pitcher.

If the ball were set spinning in the opposite direction, it would be an OUTSIDE curve. It would break *away* from a right-handed batter. This is the usual curve of right-handed pitchers. Other spins using a horizontal axis will produce curves that rise or fall.

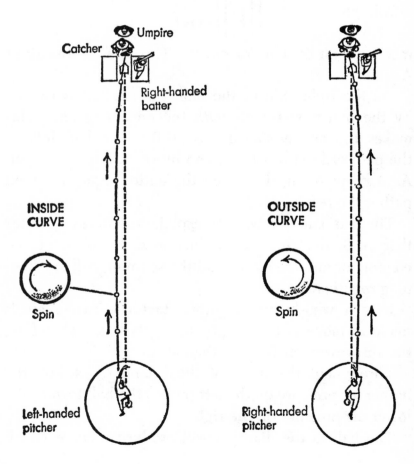

Practically all throws made by major-league pitchers are curves, in one way or another. A pitcher with straight fast balls would not be in business long.

Even the so-called fast ball is released from the pitcher's fingers with a back spin. (See illustration.) The axis of the spinning ball is horizontal. The ball crosses the plate with a rise called a HOP.

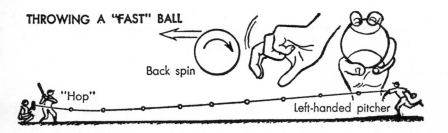

THROWING A "FAST" BALL
Back spin
"Hop"
Left-handed pitcher

Pitchers can also make a ball curve down over the plate. This is done by giving the ball an overhand spin on a horizontal axis. This is called a DROP or an OVERHAND curve.

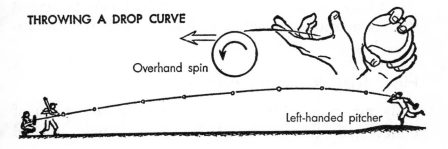

THROWING A DROP CURVE
Overhand spin
Left-handed pitcher

31

## Can a pitched ball change direction suddenly?

Many players and spectators insist that certain balls come from the pitcher in a straight line. Then, just before they reach home plate, the balls curve. Fanciful tales are told of balls which swerve left and right, loop the loop, hook, and corkscrew! Some even seem to hang in the air for an instant!

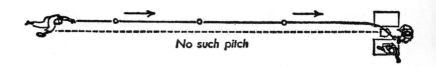

No such pitch

However, there is not a bit of scientific evidence that this occurs. No pitcher can make fast balls curve only at home plate by some kind of remote control.

Every curve is a gradual curve which starts as the ball leaves the pitcher. The batter sees only the continuation of this pitch.

But even reliable observers insist that they see the ball curve "just before home plate." The explanation may be that objects and movements appear smaller when they are farther away. The batter may be seeing the curve suddenly get larger as the ball rapidly approaches.

## How fast is a fast ball?

By means of instruments used to test the speed of bullets and other small objects, scientists have learned that fast pitchers can throw a ball about 90 to 100 miles per hour.

Bob Feller, one of the fastest pitchers of all time, could throw a ball 98.6 miles per hour. He could move his hand from back to front for such a pitch in one-eighth of a second.

## Weather, altitude, and pitching

Some pitchers feel that on hot, muggy days their curves are not as good as those on cool, dry days. They also believe that hot days are excellent for making the speediest pitches.

As you know, the air around us is not the same at all times. You hear weather reports stating that the air pressure varies from day to day.

Actually, on cool, dry days the air is heavier and more dense than on hot, humid days. The heavier the air, the greater is the resistance to baseballs moving through it. The thinner the air, the easier it is for a pitched ball to move through it.

The success of a curve depends upon the differences in air pressure set up on different parts of the spinning ball. When the air is thinner, the air pressures around the ball are decreased. This causes poor curves.

But on cool, dry days when the air is "thicker," the spinning ball develops a larger difference in pressure. Better curves are produced.

Pitchers also say that they pitch poorer curves in Denver, Colorado than they do in New York City. This is because the altitude of Denver is almost 1 mile above that of New York City, which is at sea level! The air is "thinner" in Denver.

However, while curves may be poorer in Denver, balls travel much faster because there is less air to get in the way of the balls. A pitcher can throw faster. But when a ball is hit, it travels farther too!

## Pitching distances for softball

Perhaps you would like to know the distance between the pitcher and the batter in softball, which has become a very popular sport. To make the game competitive, the pitching distance is much less than in baseball.

That is because a softball is about 3 inches larger in circumference than a baseball. It is also about 1 ounce heavier. Besides, the pitcher must use an underhand motion. That is, he pitches from below the hip.

The official pitching distance is 46 feet for men; 38 feet for women.

## Batting the ball

Every craftsman knows a great deal about the tools of his trade. A carpenter gives careful thought to selection of a new hammer. A mechanic ponders over the choice of a wrench for a certain job.

A baseball player too, learns all about the apparatus he uses to display his special talents before thousands of fans. Witness the large rack of assorted bats used by big-league players. See the deliberation that goes into the selection of the proper bat. Some players have over two dozen bats just for their personal use. No doubt you too have a favorite bat.

Batting skill is one of the biggest talents baseball players can possess. That is why they spend long hours of practice in perfecting this ability.

As you will see, there is much science involved in "swatting" the ball correctly.

## The bat

Bats are made of northern white ash grown in Pennsylvania and New York. Hickory, which is a slightly heavier wood, is also used a great deal. These trees are used because they produce wood which has the proper grain and strength as well as weight.

The rules state that no bat shall be more than 2¾ inches at its thickest point. No bat can be more than 42 inches long. Actually, most bats used in big leagues are between 34 and 35 inches in length. However, little-league bats are never more than 33 inches long.

Sometimes a bat is referred to by weight. However, the weight and size may have the same number, because a bat weighs about 1 ounce for each inch of length.

If the bat is very long, it is hard to whip it around because of inertia. But, as you learned, a heavier bat develops more momentum and consequently makes the ball travel faster and farther.

Players show their personal preference for certain bats. Some like to use lightweight bats against fast-ball pitchers. Heavier bats are swung against those pitchers who are not so fast. On hot days, or near the end of a game, lighter bats may be preferred. For those who tend to overswing, using a heavier bat may cure this fault. Some choose bats for reasons which are strictly sentimental.

## Care of the bat

Good players do not abuse their bats. They avoid striking home plate or the earth with them. Bats are not left out in the rain. Moisture warps the wood and raises the grain.

Some players rub their bats with a smooth bone in

order to flatten the grain. Oil is often rubbed on the wood after it gets wet and also when the bats are put away for a long time.

Bats should be stored over the winter in a cool, dry place, and kept in a vertical position. One way is to hang a bat from the beams in a dry cellar. Tie a string to a small nail or screw eye in the end of the handle.

The bat should not strike the ball with the "flat of the grain." The manufacturer has placed his trademark over this weak section deliberately. Players are advised to always keep the trademark up. That is, toward the sky. This will lessen the danger of splitting the bat. It will also cause less sting to the hands.

## Why bats sometimes sting

Every player knows that there is one best spot for hitting a ball the greatest distance. When a ball is hit "on the button," there is an unmistakable clear, solid sound. And the bat does not sting the hands.

You can find this spot in any bat by holding the bat horizontally in one hand. Now pick up a hammer or piece of wood and strike the bat at points 1 inch apart. Start from the heavier end of the bat. (Do not spoil your bat by denting it.)

You will find one small area which gives the most solid ring to your impact. The hand holding the bat does not feel any vibration or sting. Mark this spot.

You can repeat this experiment using both hands on the bat handle. Use your regular grip. Have a friend tap the bat with the hammer.

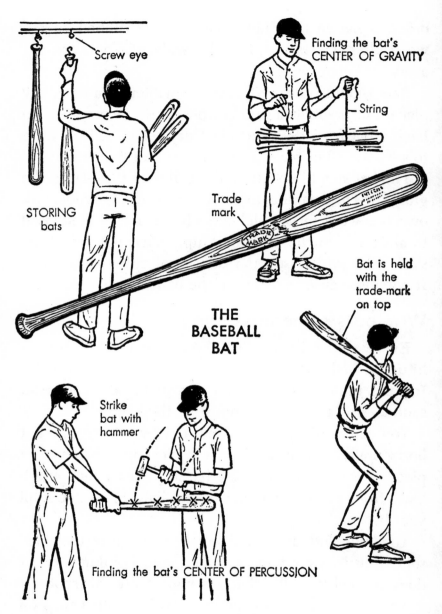

Screw eye

STORING bats

Finding the bat's CENTER OF GRAVITY

String

Trade mark

THE BASEBALL BAT

Bat is held with the trade-mark on top

Strike bat with hammer

Finding the bat's CENTER OF PERCUSSION

You have found the bat's CENTER OF PERCUSSION. It is the spot where the momentum of the batter's swing is best transferred to the ball. It is usually between 2 inches and 10 inches from the thick end of the bat.

If the ball is struck above or below this point, the bat tries to swing around this point. This twisting force tries to wrench the bat out of the hands. Actually, it is a series of back-and-forth movements called OSCILLATIONS (oss-ih-LAY-shonz). *This is what makes the bat sting.*

The farther away from the center of percussion that the bat hits the ball, the greater the twisting or vibrating effect. That is why a "handle hit" stings the hands badly and often splits the bat.

When a bat stings, the ball does not travel its maximum distance. That is because some energy is wasted while the bat is being twisted.

Many people make the error of calling the spot you have found, the center of gravity of the bat. *This is not so.*

The center of gravity is the spot where the weight of the entire bat seems to be concentrated. It can be found by suspending a bat horizontally from a string tied at different places until the bat is balanced.

The center of gravity is where the string is now tied to the bat. Mark it. You will find that this point is *not* the same as the one you found when you held the bat and struck it.

Incidentally—have you discovered that bats sting more in cold weather? Also, can you devise an experiment to show that the heavier the bat, the less will be the sting?

## About baseballs

When a bat hits a baseball, the ball is squeezed out of shape for a tiny fraction of a second. As the ball goes back to its original shape, it acts like a spring and pushes against the bat.

Reaction now sends the ball *away* from the bat. This, in addition to the momentum which the bat gives it, sends the ball out to the field.

To have any kind of order in big-league baseball, it is necessary that all balls bounce or rebound equally. They must also be alike in every other way.

After much experimentation through the years, the regulations now state that a baseball must measure between 9 and 9¼ inches in circumference. It must also weigh not less than 5 or more than 5¼ ounces.

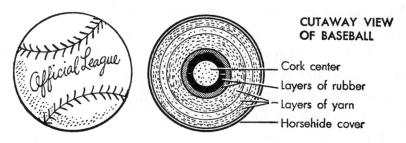

CUTAWAY VIEW OF BASEBALL

— Cork center
— Layers of rubber
— Layers of yarn
— Horsehide cover

Each ball contains a cork center covered by a layer of rubber. Various layers of cotton and woolen yarn are then wrapped evenly around the core. (See illustration.) The ball is covered by two strips of white horsehide, tightly hand-sewn by exactly 108 stitches. (No machine has ever been perfected which can properly sew on the odd-shaped, horsehide covering.)

When extreme attention is paid to all details, every ball, tested and passed, has the same "bounce."

When many home runs are hit in one season, the agitated fans are firm believers that the ball has been made more lively. But the manufacturers, just as firmly, state that today's baseball is exactly the same as the one used in 1927. That was when Babe Ruth hit sixty homers in a season of 154 games. (Nowadays, the baseball season contains 162 games.)

Every ball also has the weight perfectly distributed from its center. This makes the ball rotate evenly. If the ball were off-center it would wobble when pitched or hit. Off-center balls are often sold for fun in novelty shops. They are called CRAZY-BALLS.

Balls cannot be intentionally discolored, damaged, or moistened in any way. See how the umpire examines every ball which is foul-tipped or which strikes the net or fence. Scuffed balls are immediately replaced. Even the smallest scuff can make a pitched ball act "crazy."

A ball which is very cold loses some of its bounce, because the enclosed molecules do not move as quickly as when they are warm. When the sport was not so highly regulated, old-time pitchers used to keep the baseball in a refrigerator before a game. This deadened the bounce, and if struck, the ball would not travel far!

## Batter up!

Notice that when the batter waits for the throw he is not in a very erect position. Instead, he is slightly stooped. The reason for this stance is that it is the most natural position he can take. It is the best way one can prepare the many muscles of the body for the awaited fast swing.

It is not an easy task to overcome the inertia of a motionless bat and to build up a very high speed in two-fifths of a second. This is the approximate time it takes for a ball to reach home plate after it is released by the pitcher.

To make things more difficult, the batter wishes to get a long swing, so he holds the bat far back. In addition, he has to start his swing *before* the ball is over the plate. No wonder his tensed muscles have pulled him into the familiar batter's crouch. His body is now wound up like a spring.

Did you ever consider that this crouched position is a disadvantage to the pitcher? The strike zone is now smaller than when the batter is erect.

Crouching may also give the batter a slightly better view of the approaching ball. He is now several inches closer to the flight path of the ball.

What else does the batter use to get more force into his swing? Can you see how he steps *into* the pitch? In this way he uses his weight to help his swing. The batter stands with his side facing the pitcher. When he swings, he will turn his body around. His twisting body acts like a huge rubber band to give the bat more speed.

At every swing, try to pay particular attention to just one muscle of the batter. For instance, first study the part played by the back muscles. Then observe the leg muscles. Also those of the arms, feet, neck, fingers, and other muscles.

If you look carefully, you will see the important use of the wrist muscles. See how they snap the bat around for that extra speed.

It is also interesting to see how different batters follow through—especially after misses. A well-trained batter will follow through his swing so that he will be in a good running position to first base.

Next time you are up at bat, try to analyze your own batting style. It may be a revelation to you.

THE BAT GIVES ITS MOMENTUM TO THE BALL

## Momentum and batting

As you learned before, momentum represents the "oomph" of a moving object. This is a combination of the speed and the weight.

Scientists say that momentum cannot be destroyed. When one body gains momentum some other body loses an equal amount. When you hit a baseball with a bat, the bat slows down and gives its momentum to the ball. The momentum the ball gains is about the same as the momentum the bat loses.

## Batting fast balls

Everybody knows that fast-pitched balls are batted back to the field faster than regular pitches.

The reason is that the harder a ball hits the bat, the more it is squeezed out of shape. As it goes back to its original round condition, it gives the bat an additional push.

According to the laws of reaction, the bat pushes back equally hard in the direction of the field. This additional force increases the ball's speed and therefore its momentum. This momentum, of course, is in addition to that which the bat gives the ball.

You can prove that there is more reaction against fast balls. Simply throw a slow ball against a brick wall. Then throw a fast ball. See how the wall pushes it back faster then the slower ball.

The bat is like the brick wall. But here the "brick wall" is also coming toward the ball!

## Placing hits

The oldest advice to batters is, "Hit 'em where they ain't." As you know, players usually try to hit a ball into an unguarded or weak position.

There are many delicate conditions which determine where a ball will go after it is batted out. It is quite a complicated matter. Baseball players spend many years of study and practice trying to perfect their placement of hits. Even after many years, they cannot be absolutely certain where their hits will fall. This is what makes a baseball game so full of enjoyable suspense.

However, despite all complications, there are certain things a batter can do in order to direct his hits.

In general, the placement of a hit depends upon:
1. *The position and direction of the bat.*
   A well-hit ball will move in the direction that the bat is moving at the moment of impact.
2. *The part of the ball being struck.*

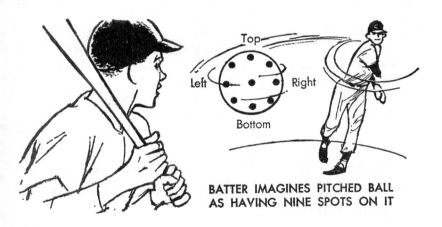

BATTER IMAGINES PITCHED BALL
AS HAVING NINE SPOTS ON IT

Consider the ball as having nine spots as it comes toward the plate.
   a. If any lower spot is struck, the ball will go upward as it leaves the batter.
   b. If any upper spot is struck, the ball will go downward.

45

c. If the center spot is struck, the ball will be batted neither up nor down. That is, it will go straight ahead.

d. Hitting any right spot will make the ball go to the left.

e. Hitting any left spot will make the ball go to the right.

Here are the possibilities:

| Spot on ball hit by bat | General direction where the ball will go |
|---|---|
| Upper center | grounder toward pitcher |
| Middle center | straight ahead toward pitcher |
| Lower center | toward pitcher, but over his head |
| Upper left | grounder to right field |
| Middle left | straight ahead to right field |
| Lower left | fly ball to right field |
| Upper right | grounder to left field |
| Middle right | straight ahead to left field |
| Lower right | fly ball to left field |

Actually, when the batter changes the position and direction of his bat, he is selecting the spot on the ball which he wishes to hit.

In other words, suppose he strikes the ball when his bat is at right angles (perpendicular, 90 degrees) to the path of the pitched ball. Then all balls will very probably go *toward* the pitcher, because he is hitting the center of the ball.

In this position the bat can hit the upper, lower, or middle center of the ball.

46

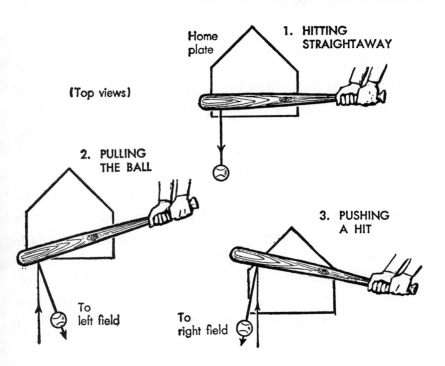

**1. HITTING STRAIGHTAWAY**

Home plate

(Top views)

**2. PULLING THE BALL**

**3. PUSHING A HIT**

To left field

To right field

## Pulling and pushing hits

In order to keep the ball from going straight in the direction of the pitcher, the bat's position must be changed.

If a right-handed batter meets the ball out in front of him, his bat will be in a position to send the ball to left field. (See illustration.) If a left-handed batter meets the ball in front of him he will hit to right field.

Such batters are called PULL HITTERS. The most powerful hitters are pull hitters because they throw the weight of the entire body into the swing giving the bat more momentum. They also exert maximum force because their muscles are *pulling* the bat to them. Another feature is that pulling a hit allows for a longer swing because the batter starts his swing early. The longer the swing, the greater is the momentum of the bat.

When a right-handed batter wishes to hit to right field he must change his timing so that he swings late. Consequently when he hits the ball at a point behind his position at the plate, he is pushing his hit to right field. A left-handed batter will push a hit to left field.

Pushing a hit usually results in a weak hit. The position of the player's body does not allow him to use his muscles to full advantage. He uses a pushing or slapping action as he hits the ball.

There is another reason for a pusher's weak swing. He has to meet the ball late. This gives him little time to speed up his swing. His bat does not develop much momentum.

## Bunting

Bunting is a spectacular bit of baseball strategy. At the moment of bunting, the batter holds his bat loosely and horizontally. One hand is on the handle and the other near the trademark. He does not push at the ball. He lets the ball hit the bat.

When the ball makes contact, most of its momentum is absorbed in jarring the loosely held bat. Because the bat itself has developed very little momentum, the ball does not travel far.

Since the bunt must be to the ground (a bunted fly ball is fatal!), the best pitch is a low ball. This allows the batter to hit the top of the ball.

The pitcher may suspect that a bunt is coming. He will try to throw a high strike.

## Catching, fielding, and running bases

Crack! The batter has connected with the pitcher's best effort. The ball is shot to the crouching third baseman. He scoops it up with a grace that is beautiful to behold. Like a well-aimed bullet, the ball is thrown to the outstretched hands of the first baseman.

An instant later the runner races across first base. The umpire signifies that the runner is out, a victim of the rule that there shall be 90 feet between bases. That is the distance which a runner has great difficulty in reaching, especially when the opposing team is highly efficient.

Any wasted motion, or a momentary fumble, would have made the runner safe. Baseball players know the value of split-seconds when fielding hits or running bases. That is why they use science to help them in every way.

In order to make little-league baseball competitive, it was necessary to set 60 feet as the official distance between all bases. Experiments with various longer and shorter distances showed that one side or the other was getting too great an advantage.

## About gloves

Gloves are used mainly to protect the hands of the players. The momentum developed by a 5-ounce ball traveling at 85 miles per hour can cause an annoying sting.

One of the reasons that a glove reduces the impact is because it has padding. There are many kinds of padding, but usually a specially prepared felt is used.

The springlike nature of the padding, and the leather, force the ball to take a longer time to slow down. This reduces the shock of impact. For the same reason, the player also brings his hands back at the instant he catches a fast ball.

Another reason why a glove reduces sting is that it spreads the impact over a larger area. Notice in the first illustration how a bare hand catches a fast ball. Here the impact area is only where the ball touches the skin. The full force is acting over a small area. Therefore, the sting is great.

Now see in the second illustration how the tough leather of a glove helps spread this force over a larger section of the enclosed hand. One spot does not get the

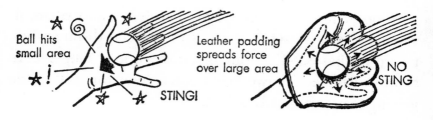

Ball hits small area

STING!

Leather padding spreads force over large area

NO STING

full impact as with a bare hand. This removes most of the sting.

Many years ago baseball players used no gloves. Later, it was found that gloves caught and held balls better. Soon fielders were using netlike affairs which trapped fly balls like butterflies.

That is why official rules today are very definite about sizes of gloves. Even the space between the thumb section and the finger section is given very specifically for different gloves. However, the catcher may use any size, weight, or shape he wishes.

Little-leaguers' gloves are the same kind used in big leagues except that they are in smaller sizes.

## The catcher is an important player

The catcher is usually one of the huskiest players on the team. His job calls for more strength and stamina than that needed by other players.

He is the quarterback of his team. As the only player who can see all his teammates at one time, he often holds up a game until everyone is in the proper position. He can slow down or speed up a game simply by how soon he returns the ball to the pitcher.

The catcher constantly watches the stance of a batter. This is often a giveaway of the kind of a ball the batter intends to hit.

For example, a batter may be standing too close to the plate. The catcher signals to the pitcher for a high inside pitch, since such batters can hit an outside ball very hard.

Observe that the catcher does not receive the pitch in a full squat position. Instead, he stands half-erect, on the balls of his feet, and with his body bent forward. This enables him to throw a ball to a baseman with little loss of motion.

A catcher with a good arm and aim is "instant death" for anyone trying to steal a base. For example, suppose a runner tries to steal second base. The catcher will usually throw the ball to the left knee of the second baseman. This is the best trajectory for a tag.

Watch a catcher go after a high fly ball to the rear of home plate. He usually throws his mask in the opposite direction to where he is moving. This prevents his tripping over it. Such pop-ups are hard to catch, especially with a heavily padded glove and while wearing his protective devices. The ball may be coming down very close to the dugout, screen, or grandstand. The catcher who is looking up, may hurt himself by running into one of these.

Foul balls usually have a peculiar trajectory because of the spin given the ball as it skids off the bat. Some balls may even curve back toward home plate like a boomerang. The wind also produces tricky behavior when a ball has a high spin on it.

## Watch the fielders

Once in a while a fielder has to make a spectacular jump. Sometimes he thrills the bleacher fans with a successful do-or-die catch.

But in the main, every fielder who has learned his

business well, has a definite routine for catching fly balls.

First, he considers what kind of a hitter is at bat. Watch how he shifts his location to be better able to receive the expected hit. For example, he knows whether the batter is a pull or a push hitter. He is often tipped off by the way the batter stands.

The fielder begins his pursuit at the crack of the bat. Years of experience have taught him to estimate the trajectory of a fly ball. He runs to where the ball will probably fall. Very often his back is to the ball. When he turns to face the ball usually he has to make only small adjustments to catch it. Once in a while, a fielder only has to back up to get under the ball.

Remember that in the outfield the ball is not traveling as fast as when it was struck. For example, when a fly ball is first hit it may be going close to 100 miles an hour.

Measurements show that it reaches a fielder 294 feet away in 4.3 seconds. That is an average speed of 47 miles per hour. So you can see how quickly speed tapers off.

Outfielders must always know the direction and strength of the wind. They look at the stadium's flags, at chimney smoke, or toss grass into the air. They allow for the wind when estimating where the ball will fall. It is better for the wind to carry the ball *to* the fielders than *away* from them. Sometimes they call for a nearby fielder to take the catch.

Observe how most fielders run on the balls of their feet and do not step down hard on their heels. In this way they do not jar their bodies or their eyes. If they ran any other way they would see the ball bobbing up and down. Try it yourself. It may take a little practice to do this properly.

There is a technique for catching a fly ball when it is in danger of getting lost in the sun. First, the fielder places his glove overhead so that the sun is blocked from view.

The ball is watched carefully until it goes into the sun. The ball is *not* watched while it travels across the sun. This would temporarily blind the player long enough for him to lose the ball.

The ball is caught sight of as it comes out from behind the glove covering the sun.

Today most fielders use polaroid sunglasses. These cut out glare and also help the fielder follow a ball which may have very little contrast against gray cloudy skies.

## The science of throwing

A good ball player must know how, when, and where to throw a ball.

Without natural muscle development a ball player can never become a very fast thrower. But every player can obtain extra speed by learning how to use leverage, momentum, reaction, friction, air pressure, and other factors.

Most throwers are taught to give the ball a backward rotation such as a pitcher uses in throwing a fast ball.

See page 31. This rotation makes the ball go farther in the air and also will make it bounce straight.

One of the secrets of returning a ball quickly is to be set for it. See how the infield players are usually low

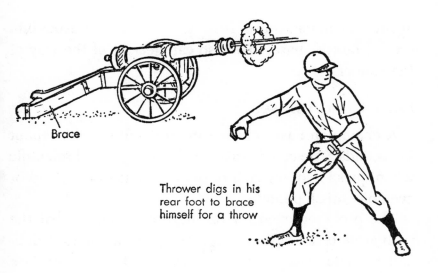

Brace

Thrower digs in his rear foot to brace himself for a throw

and bent forward. They catch the ball and throw it with just one step in any direction. If they had to straighten out their bodies to throw they would lose a fraction of a second. See how a fielder scoops up a ball and is immediately in position for a throw.

A low trajectory is a timesaver when throwing a ball for speed. Getting the arm high and making a large arc will also increase speed. A strong elbow and wrist snap are also in order.

Watch how a thrower digs his rear foot into the ground when he wants speed or distance. He uses the same principle of reaction as a cannon which is braced in the rear. (See illustration.) The braced rear foot and the braced cannon allow a harder backward push to be given the ground. The reaction forward then becomes greater.

A first baseman saves a split-second by stepping *toward* the ball thrown to him. He does this by pushing against the infield side of first base.  Reaction pushes him away from the base.  He also can get out of the way of the runner.

## How to run bases

A champion base runner can circle all bases in about 14 seconds.  He can do this only by using sound scientific techniques.  Not an inch of distance must be wasted or even one misstep made.

The problem, even for the fastest runner, is that the path around the bases is angular.  Inertia makes it difficult to make sharp turns.  It is easier to continue in a straight line.

If a runner follows a direct line to a base, his inertia will carry him along a wide arc toward the next base. The larger the arc, the greater the distance he must run.

Expert runners have found that it is best to make most of the turn *before* coming to the base.  The illustration on page 57 shows how to save valuable seconds when running to second base.

A runner uses another trick when rounding bases.  He hits the *inside* corner of the base with one leg and pushes hard toward the next base.  Either leg can be used as long as he does not break his stride.  However, if possible, it is best to use the left leg.  Many coaches feel that this leg gives the best fast turn and push-off.

According to the principle of reaction, the harder a runner pushes the base, the harder the base pushes him toward the next one.

A player also saves split-seconds by starting for first

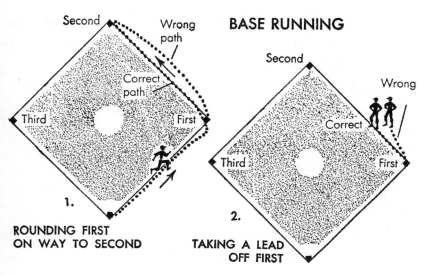

**1. ROUNDING FIRST ON WAY TO SECOND**

**2. TAKING A LEAD OFF FIRST**

base as soon as he hits the ball. He tries to be in a good position to overcome his inertia quickly.

Notice how a runner always uses his body to help him round a base. He leans in toward the pitcher and lowers his left shoulder. He also swings his right arm toward the next base.

## "Hitting the dirt"

Many people have the wrong idea about sliding into bases. They think that this gives a runner a sudden increase of speed in order to beat the ball to the base. Actually, sliding slows down a player.

A fast runner cannot stop suddenly. He therefore slides to prevent his inertia from carrying him past a base and causing him to be tagged.

The only base a player can overrun legally is first base. That is why players do not slide into this bag.

Friction of the body against the earth slows down the runner. Contrary to popular belief, the spikes are not supposed to be in the ground.

The runner "hits the dirt" about 10 to 15 feet before a base. He has various techniques for giving the baseman a small target for tagging.

## Stealing bases

There is more to stealing bases than simply trying to beat the ball to the base. It is a skill involving much practice. It calls for a study of psychology in trying to outguess the pitcher. It takes into account certain facts in science.

Consider these:

    a. A fast ball is thrown 120 feet per second.

    b. A fast runner travels 30 feet per second.

    c. It takes three-fourths of one second for the catcher to throw a ball to second base.

You can see that a thrown ball is four times as fast as a runner. It would be foolish for a player to try to beat a ball.

He cannot even run to second if the catcher is holding the ball! It would take him three seconds of very fast running to cover the distance of 90 feet. Add at least another second for his inertia in getting started and for stopping. His total time from first base to second base would be at least four seconds.

But the catcher can throw from home plate to second base in about one-fourth the time!

So you see, the only way for a runner to steal a base is

to be cunning. *He must take a lead.* Or he can start running while the ball is in play. But at no time must he compete on an even basis with a thrown ball. If he does, then he is a "dead duck"!

An experienced stealer observes different parts of the pitcher's body. He can tell within a fraction of a second when the pitcher is starting a real pitching motion. He may also know when a "pick-off" throw is being considered by the pitcher.

It is interesting to note that the pitcher's throw to first is not always made to catch the runner off base. The main purpose of the throw is to prevent the runner from getting the lead which he so urgently needs.

Once in a while a runner is "caught in a run-down." That is, he is trapped between two bases. He runs up and back to avoid being tagged. In big leagues, this almost always ends in disaster for the runner. In only several throws, the runner learns that you cannot beat the ball.

Frequently, during a run-down, the runner is made to commit himself. The man with the ball *pretends* to throw. The runner starts running and cannot change his direction in time.

Notice that the throwing arm is always held high. This makes it ready to throw the ball and puts the ball in a spot where the other fielder can see it. In a short distance, the ball can be thrown too fast for him to see it in time. It may even hit his face.

## Baseball is going modern

Everything in our country is in tune with this wonderful electronic era in which we are living. It is natural that baseball too should use modern ideas. Bit by bit, we find that conditions in this sport, which we have always been taking for granted, are being changed.

This chapter should help you realize that things keep changing all the time! Especially when scientists and technicians put their minds to problems.

## Radio and television

Today you can always be within earshot of a good baseball game. You can use your radio set at home or in an automobile. Or you can take a walk while you are tuned in on your transistorized pocket-size portable!

It is also a joy to see a sizzling game on television. For only a few cents, which you pay for the electricity, you can have "the best seat in the stadium." And you also get the free comments from top experts in the game.

TV cameras are set up at the field to quickly cover all possible plays in the game. Some cameras have special lenses which can follow a player and keep him in constant focus. They are called ZOOMAR lenses.

Formerly, the camera man had to use one of several lenses. These were mounted on a holder which would swing the proper lens into place. Some lenses were used for close-ups of the batter or pitcher. Others were for distant actions. Zoomar lenses have made life simpler for TV cameramen.

Five TV cameras are usually used to cover every angle of the field as follows:

a. Two cameras are set up in the press box behind home plate. They make a direct line with home plate and the pitcher. More often, they are slightly to one side.

b. One camera is in the bleachers, usually behind the people. It may be in a direct line with the pitcher and home plate. But usually, it is a little to one side.

c. One TV camera is set up in the stands along the first base line.

d. Another camera, also in the stands, covers the third base line.

In the TV booth there is a screen for each camera. It is called a MONITOR. The director can see what picture each camera is taking. He selects the picture he wants on the air by turning switches.

He also has two more monitors for his commercials. These are often sent from the main studio.

You can see games originating in other cities. Also, if you miss a game there is a chance that you can see it an-

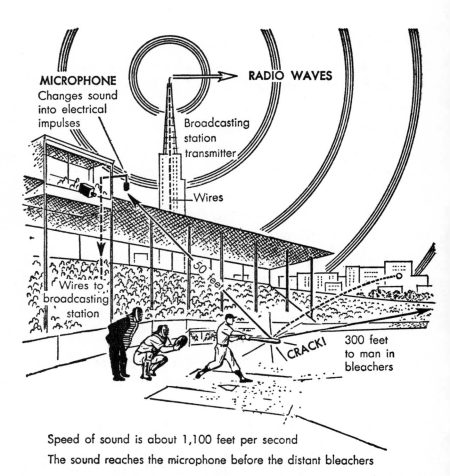

**MICROPHONE**
Changes sound
into electrical
impulses

**RADIO WAVES**

Broadcasting
station
transmitter

Wires

Wires to
broadcasting
station

50 feet

CRACK!

300 feet
to man in
bleachers

Speed of sound is about 1,100 feet per second
The sound reaches the microphone before the distant bleachers

other time. Television can be recorded on special **tape**
and played back.

## You hear sounds sooner at home

Suppose a player bats a ball at the stadium. Do you
know that you hear the sound *at home* before many people hear it in the bleachers?

Sound travels in air about 1,100 feet per second. Spectators in the bleachers are hundreds of feet away from

AERIAL

So you hear the sound at home before the man in the bleachers does

The speed of electricity in wires and air is almost instantaneous

CRACK!

the batter. It takes a fraction of a second for them to hear the sound. But even though you may be 10 miles away, you hear the sound before they do.

The microphone for radio or TV is placed near home plate. The sound is changed to electrical impulses. These travel through the air to your set at the speed of light, which is 186,000 miles per second.

Your set changes the electrical impulses back to sound vibrations. The loud speaker sends these to your ear.

The sound only travels through air for a *short* distance at home. It has to travel a *long* distance at the stadium. You can disregard the time the impulse traveled through all the electronic equipment and through space to your home. The time is practically instantaneous.

## Turning night into day

When you go to a night baseball game you are witnessing a modern miracle. The light is so bright you can follow the ball and the plays very comfortably. Yet you are not annoyed by glare. That is because the groups

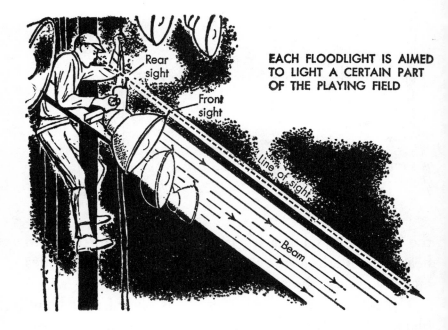

Rear sight

Front sight

EACH FLOODLIGHT IS AIMED TO LIGHT A CERTAIN PART OF THE PLAYING FIELD

Line of sight

Beam

of floodlights are on poles about 120 feet high. Each reflector is aimed at a certain spot on the field determined by illumination engineers. The aiming device is like the two sights on a rifle.

Notice that the lights are placed so that they do not shine directly into the players' eyes. They are never along base lines, or in a direct line with the pitcher and catcher. Also observe that the players do not cast any strong shadows.

The infield is where much fast action occurs. Therefore it has 1½ times the illumination of the outfield. By using instruments similar to your photography exposure meter, engineers have determined that the light at a night baseball game is equal to that of about 4,000 full moons.

Most large baseball parks have over a thousand lamps,

each 1,500 watts. That means over 1½ million watts are being used! Compare that with your reading lamp, which is probably 75 watts.

In many parks the lamps operate at a slightly higher voltage than they were designed for. It has been found that in this way they give one-third more light. But— you guessed it—the bulbs burn out faster.

## Iron Mike—the pitching machine

Years ago, spring training meant tired arms for pitchers. They had to provide their teammates with an endless number of pitches for batting practice. Today, all big teams save their pitchers' strength by using some form of Iron Mike.

This is the nickname given to the different kinds of modern pitching machines. One of the first of these automatic machines was also called OVERHAND JOE.

These machines are usually electrically operated as follows: Many balls are loaded into the machines at one time. A single baseball is fed into the end of a long arm.

As the arm is raised by a motor, it also winds up a powerful spring. (Some use a heavy rubber band.) At exactly the proper moment, the arm trips a release, and the spring brings the arm quickly forward. The ball, held in loose jaws, is thrown to the batter.

The machines are amazingly accurate. They are adjustable for throwing high and low strikes, inside or outside. Many also pitch change-of-pace balls. Some even deliver curves. They can be operated by the coach, or made to pitch automatically at about seven balls per min-

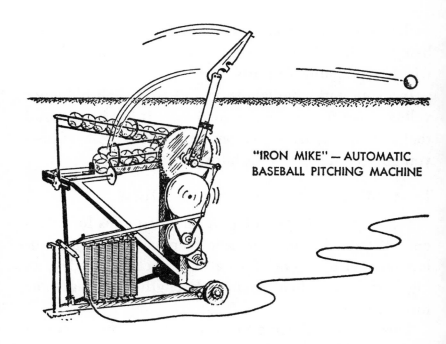

"IRON MIKE" — AUTOMATIC
BASEBALL PITCHING MACHINE

ute. Speeds can be increased up to about 98 miles per hour.

Balls roll back to the operator of the machine. There is no need for a catcher. Many machines have a novel pipeline system for having the fly balls returned to them from the field.

One kind of machine uses compressed air for sending out the balls. It is aptly called the BAZOOKA. Such machines are often used to throw balls high overhead. They give catchers practice in snaring high fouls.

Many amusement parks or carnivals have batting ranges set up. You may see Iron Mikes in action there. You can bat out nine balls for about a quarter.

Automatic pitching machines cost from $200 to $1,000.

Remote control
operator

## Automatic umpire

Slow motion movies have proved that umpires of big leagues call them right 99 times in 100. Nevertheless, an engineer recently patented an electronic umpire which has a much better average. In fact, it is never wrong.

It consists of three television cameras so located that balls and strikes can be determined from them. One is set up so that it gets an overhead view of home plate. This is in back of the plate, but in a direct line with the pitcher and home plate.

Another camera is set up on the right side of the batter. It is adjustable for the batter's strike zone. There is also another camera set up on the left for left-handed batters.

These cameras send their impulses by wire to two television monitors in the umpire's booth. The umpire can

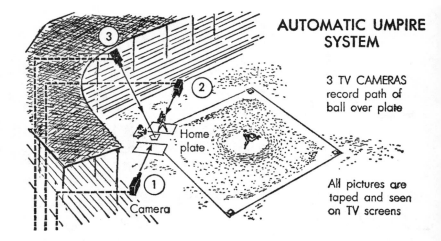

## AUTOMATIC UMPIRE SYSTEM

3 TV CAMERAS
record path of
ball over plate

Home
plate

All pictures are
taped and seen
on TV screens

Camera

easily tell whether a ball is crossing the plate. He can also see clearly whether a ball is between the knees and armpits. This screen contains adjustable horizontal markers for this.

Every pitch is taped and stored as an electronic memory. Any section of a pitch can be played back, over and over again. The ball can be made to "freeze" on the TV screen.

This setup can also be used for pitching practice. Some arrangement can be made whereby the pitcher

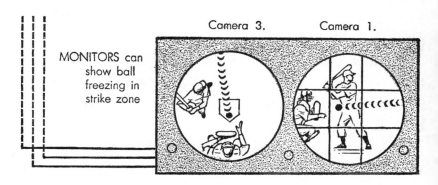

Camera 3.      Camera 1.

MONITORS can
show ball
freezing in
strike zone

can tell the effect of his pitch.  Also, what correction is needed to improve it.

Any base on the diamond may be monitored in the same way.  The TV cameras can be placed so that every angle of the base is covered.  Long distance (telephoto) lenses would be used to enlarge the action.

## How is bounce of a baseball tested?

A compressed air gun shoots a ball toward a steel plate. On the way to the steel plate the ball passes a velocity testing device.

When the ball strikes the steel plate, it bounces back. As it does this, it passes the velocity tester again.  The faster it moves when it rebounds, the greater the ball's liveliness.

This method can be used to make sure that all balls used in games are the same.

## Pinch-hitters

Sometimes when an opposing pitcher is right-handed, the manager will substitute a pinch-hitter who is left-handed.

One of the reasons is that a right-handed pitcher causes the ball to spin so that it curves *away* from the right-handed batter.  It also curves *toward* a left-handed batter.

It is usually harder for a batter to hit a ball breaking *away* from him than one which is breaking *toward* him. Therefore, a left-handed batter finds it easier to hit a right-handed pitcher's curve.

## Right-handed infielders

Look carefully at all the infield players. You will probably find that all of them are right-handed.

Most infield work, especially throwing to first base, is best done by right-handed throwers. The first-baseman can be either right- or left-handed.

## Saving precious moments

Watch a right-handed fielder's foot. He catches a ball with his left foot already forward. This puts him into a throwing position immediately.

Try throwing a ball hard with your right foot forward. Your muscles will not allow this.

Of course, a left-handed fielder puts his right foot forward.

## Direction of base running

Why are bases run counterclockwise, that is, opposite to the direction of clock hands?

This probably came about because most players are right-handed. It was found that the game was speeded up if first base was in a location which was easier to throw to.

Suppose bases were run clockwise? That is, if third base became first base. Do you see that then it would be better if all infield players were left-handed?

## Left-handed batters get head start

Watch a left-handed batter hit the ball. As his bat swings around, he is usually in a very good position to run to first base.

Now study a right-handed batter as he takes a mighty swing. His momentum and follow-through turn him partly away from first base.

He has to lose a split-second while he turns and speeds to first base.

A southpaw's pitching arm is toward the south.

## Why are left-handed pitchers called southpaws?

Large stadiums are designed so that the afternoon sun, which is in the west, is not in the eyes of the batter. It would give the pitcher too great an advantage. Besides, it would be too dangerous for the man at bat.

The official rules suggest that a line from home base through the pitcher's plate shall run in an easterly or northeasterly direction.

Therefore, when pitchers face home plate, their left hands (paws) are toward the south.

This is probably why "lefties" got to be called SOUTH-PAWS.

71

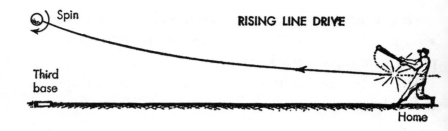

## Why a line drive often rises

Watch the path taken by a ball which is hit by the batter very hard and horizontally. A line drive gives you an excellent view because it *cuts across* your field of vision.

Frequently the ball will be seen to rise as it approaches third or first base. One of the reasons for this is that the ball was given a spin by being struck below center.

This spin is similar to the one possessed by a fast ball thrown by the pitcher. This "hop" makes the ball sail. It is actually an upward curve.

## Why do batters wear special caps?

When a batter comes to bat he puts on a protective cap. After he gets to first base he often exchanges it for his regular cap.

A player may choose to wear the first cap throughout the game. This will protect him against thrown balls, base and fence collisions.

The batter wears this stiff cap to avoid serious injury, should he be struck by a "bean" ball or a "duster" at 85 miles per hour. It is not sportsmanlike or legal for a pitcher to frighten a batter by throwing a very close ball. But accidents do happen.

72

The cap is usually made of lightweight fiberglass (spun glass). The inside has a top cushion of rubber. There is also a shock-absorbing liner.

The hard surface and shock-absorbing band spread the force of the impact. In this way, it is not concentrated in one spot.

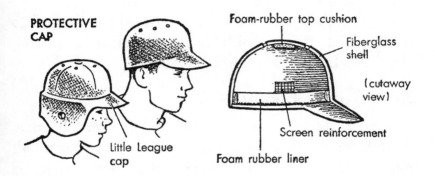

## Rosin bags

Look for a small white bag near the pitcher's mound. It is usually behind the pitcher and to one side. You may also see one near the batter's circle.

These cotton bags contain ROSIN, a substance which comes from the production of turpentine.

When the floppy bag is handled, some of the powder comes through the cloth. It is rubbed on the hands to give them a certain pleasant stickiness. This increases the friction when gripping a bat or a ball.

Rosin is used by violinists for increasing friction on the bow. It is also used in football and other sports. In boxing, it is rubbed on the shoes to increase friction against the canvas.

## Players wear sliding pads

The runner who makes his spectacular slide into a base is fairly well protected against friction burns. Underneath his uniform he wears padding usually made of quilted flannel. These protect his hips and thighs. There is extra padding at contact points.

See how the slider keeps his hands off the ground to avoid injury. He also holds his body as relaxed as he can. This helps him absorb the shock better.

## Babe Ruth's homer

The next time you see a player hit a ball over the fence, try to think of Babe Ruth's record. He once hit a ball that traveled 602 feet. Can you imagine the force needed to do this?

Every player's home run is pitiful compared to this record. No one has ever come close to this distance. For years people would visit the spot where the ball was supposed to have dropped. They could hardly see home plate clearly without binoculars.

Sportswriters like to tell of a homer that traveled even farther than Ruth's. It was hit by Ernie Lombardi of the Cincinnati Reds, for a distance of 30 miles! The ball came over the fence, and landed in a passing truck which made a delivery 30 miles away.

# FOOTBALL

## Football—game of momentum

Football is the king of autumn sports for millions of enthusiastic fans across the country. It is a spectacular game calling for thrilling action and rough physical contacts.

The purpose of the game is to advance the ball across the field by means of strategy, strength, speed, and teamwork. It is like a gigantic game of chess, calling for very careful planning. Many see it as a mimic war, with the quarterbacks as generals.

Football has a very long history, with constant changing of the rules to make the game more competitive, but at the same time to lessen the element of danger. Still the rules are aimed at keeping football rugged and full of physical contacts. This is what the players enjoy. This is what the spectators come to see.

## How to watch a football game

Most people watch only the player with the ball. This is understandable, because he seems to be the center of activity. However, a spectator can get a deeper appreciation of what is going on by learning to look for the finer points of the game.

There is more than just watching the ball carrier streaking down the field for a touchdown. See how wise planning and skillful blocking make his long run possible. Observe the faking which draws some of the opposing team away from the real action. Keep your attention on the defensive backfield players. Study their tackling attempts.

If you look at football with a scientific eye, you will realize that this is truly a game of momentum. Every example of the laws of motion is clearly and vividly demonstrated.

## Stability

Football is a game where a player is stopped in his advance by being thrown to the ground. He may have his balance upset by tackling, blocking, or by other means.

One of the most important techniques a good player learns is how to make himself less likely to be thrown over. To become a master at this, he must learn the scientific principles involved. Then he may be better able to stay put and hold his ground like the Rock of Gibraltar. At the same time, he learns to use his knowledge of science when throwing an opposing player to the ground.

The ability of a player to return to his original position when pushed or pulled is called STABILITY. An easily upset player has poor stability. One who remains on his feet and holds his ground has good stability. He is stable.

## Center of gravity

Place a ruler on your finger. You will find that it balances at the 6-inch point. This spot is called the ruler's CENTER OF GRAVITY. It is the point at which all the weight may be considered to be concentrated.

Balance a piece of cardboard or wood of irregular shape, as shown in the illustration. The balancing point is its center of gravity.

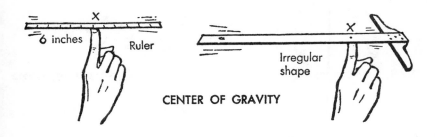

CENTER OF GRAVITY

A player too, has a center of gravity. (See page 78.) When he stands up, his center of gravity rises. When he crouches, his center of gravity becomes lower.

Experience shows that the lower the center of gravity, the greater the stability of the object. You can see examples of this all around you. A tall narrow flower vase is made more stable by pouring sand or gravel into it. Floor lamps have heavy bases. Racing automobiles are built low. Ships have low keels.

In the same way, a football player gets greater stability by crouching and making his center of gravity lower. When he raises his center of gravity he makes his stability less.

77

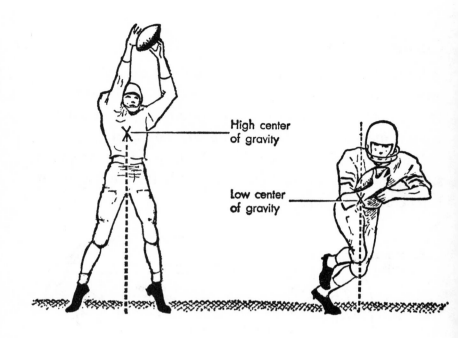

High center
of gravity

Low center
of gravity

## Making the base broad

Everybody knows that the broader the base of an object, the harder it is to tip it over. The football player tries to make as large a base as possible. (See illustrations.) He does this by spreading his legs apart and placing his hand on the ground. This is the famous 3-point stance. It gives him the stability of a tripod.

Drop an imaginary vertical line from the center of gravity of an object to the ground. If the line falls *inside* the base, the object is stable. If the center of gravity is over the *outside* of the base, the object is unstable. It will not be able to stand on that base. It will fall and land on one of its broad sides. This will become its new base.

## Importance of momentum

It is logical that the greater the impact or momentum against a player, the easier it is to throw him over.

You have learned that momentum cannot be destroyed. It can be transferred. When a bat hits a baseball, the ball acquires the momentum of the bat.

The same principle applies to the football carrier who is tackled. At impact, he gains most of the momentum of the tackler. Unfortunately, this makes him move in an unwanted direction. His center of gravity is suddenly forced to fall outside his base. He loses his stability.

Stated simply, momentum is determined by multiplying the velocity of the runner by his weight. Either fast motion or weight can be used to build up a high impact ability. See page 14. A quarterback who weighs only 150 pounds can develop a greater momentum than a 200-pound guard. But only if the quarterback is running at a greater speed.

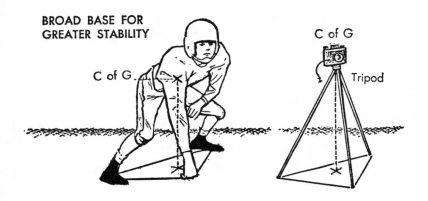

BROAD BASE FOR GREATER STABILITY

C of G

C of G

Tripod

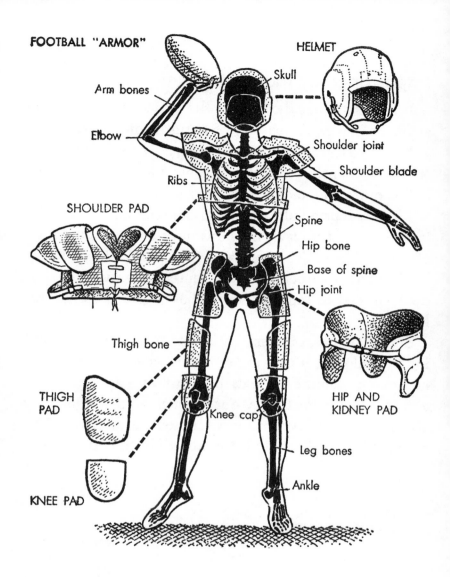

FOOTBALL "ARMOR"

HELMET

Skull

Arm bones

Elbow

Shoulder joint

Shoulder blade

Ribs

SHOULDER PAD

Spine

Hip bone

Base of spine

Hip joint

Thigh bone

THIGH PAD

HIP AND KIDNEY PAD

Knee cap

Leg bones

Ankle

KNEE PAD

## Protective uniforms

The human body is not designed by nature to be tossed around like a sack of potatoes. Nor is it able to stand, unaided, the sudden blows and falls inflicted during blocking and tackling.

80

Players protect themselves against broken bones and bruises by wearing scientifically designed pads underneath their colorful jerseys and pants. These may look bulky, but they are quite light in weight. They are made mainly of molded polyethylene plastic and are excellent shock absorbers. They also provide great freedom of movement. The knights of old would have been delighted with some of this armor.

The uniform includes a plastic helmet and pads for shoulders, hips, knees, and thighs. There are also many protective devices for other body parts.

These pads absorb and weaken the force of a blow by causing the slowing-down action to take longer. At the same time, the impact of the force is spread over a larger area underneath the armor. This results in less pressure.

Study the illustrations. They show how parts of the body are protected by football gear. Look for the parts of the skeleton which stick out slightly. These bones are easily hurt and need special protection. See page 138.

Shoulder pads protect the parts of the body which are subjected to most contact. They give special protection to the collarbone, which is very easily fractured.

This harness also protects the shoulder blades, several shoulder joints, and the ball portion of the upper arm joint. At the same time it helps prevent injuries to the back and neck.

Other heavily protected areas are the hips, kidneys, and bottom of the spine. Notice how completely the pads cover these.

Feel on your body all those parts labeled on the skeleton.

## Life-saving helmets

In the early days of football, wearing a helmet was the mark of a "sissy." Today it is the most important piece of protective equipment. Every player wears one to protect the skull, back of the head, and the ears.

Modern helmets are scientifically engineered and tested. The outside shell is made of a hard plastic. When struck, it spreads the impact over a larger surface. This reduces the shock in any one spot.

You can prove this yourself. Strike your skull with the eraser part of a pencil. Use enough force to make it annoying. Now place a stiff piece of cardboard, or a thin hard-covered book against your head.

Strike the book with the pencil held in the same way as before. Use the same part of the head and, of course, the same force. You will find that your head does not feel the annoying shock in one spot. You will also find that the pressure is decreased.

The shock is spread still farther by another method. Inside every helmet there is a suspension web consisting of bands of padded leather. These hold the head about 1 inch away from the top of the helmet.

Each band takes up its share of the impact. The result is that the force of a dangerous shock is spread over a very large area. The final pressure on any one spot cannot do serious harm.

A chin strap holds the helmet firmly in place. Many players also have face guards attached to their helmets. These may be made of extremely strong nylon.

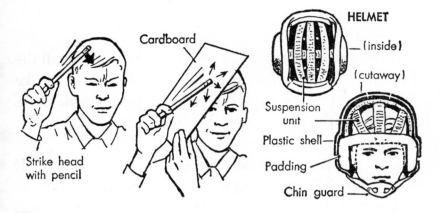

Strike head with pencil

Cardboard

HELMET

(inside)

(cutaway)

Suspension unit

Plastic shell

Padding

Chin guard

## About footballs

The first footballs were round, since football originated from a game which used a soccer ball. Today's football is egg shaped. If you like to use big words, you may call it a PROLATE SPHEROID (PROH-late-SPHEER-oid).

It is still called a PIGSKIN even though this type of leather is hardly ever used for footballs. A modern ball consists of four panels of tan-colored leather sewed together. A rubber bladder is inserted and inflated to about 13 pounds per square inch. The leather is then laced together smoothly.

The surface of the ball has a slightly dimpled finish. Some balls are given a special tacky feeling. These features help a player get a better grip, especially on rainy days.

The regulation ball weighs about 14½ ounces. It is slightly over 11 inches long. The diameter at the center is about 6¾ inches.

For better visibility the ball has two white stripes, about 1 inch wide and about 3½ inches from each end.

## Spiral passes

Do you remember how poorly you threw a football the first time? The ball went end over end—not at all like the passes made by a quarterback! It takes a little practice to give the ball a special spin as it is released from the fingertips.

The spin is what makes the ball easier to catch. It makes the ball travel faster, farther, and in a more accurate trajectory. The spin also reduces the effects of **wind** resistance which can force the football off its course.

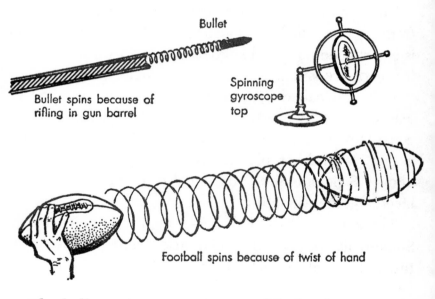

Bullet

Bullet spins because of rifling in gun barrel

Spinning gyroscope top

Football spins because of twist of hand

The ball continues to spin smoothly for the same reason that a spinning top stands upright. A toy GYROSCOPE (JEYE-ruh-scope) will also continue to rotate in any position in which it is placed. You may also compare the spin on the football with a rifle bullet. The barrel of the gun has spiral grooves in it. The bullet is set spinning so that it will go to its target accurately.

Newton's law of motion dealing with inertia states that an object in motion will continue moving in the direction it is going, unless some force causes a change.

There is a special case of inertia involving things that spin. It may be stated this way:

An object which is rotating about an axis will continue to rotate about that same axis, unless some force causes a change.

The fingers and wrist set the football rotating around the ball's long axis (from end to end). (See illustration.) Because of its inertia, the ball will continue spinning that way. It will resist any change in direction of its spinning axis. That is why the ball does not tumble end over end. The ball makes a smooth trajectory to its target.

Experts say that when the ball is released from the hand, the long axis should point at an angle of 10 to 15 degrees with the ground. This probably gives it the proper "lift" so that it sails farther. The wing of an airplane behaves in almost the same way.

Good passers change this angle when throwing with, against, or across the wind.

## Football in action

There is an imaginary battlefront extending across the field where the ball rests. It is called the SCRIMMAGE LINE. Here the struggle goes on to keep the man carrying the ball from breaking loose.

The team with the ball is called the OFFENSIVE team. Seven men of this team are at the scrimmage line. The other four players are in the rear. The defensive team can spread out its men as it sees fit.

The ball carrier is the only offensive player who can use his hands on an opponent. The others on his team can only use their bodies for stopping or warding off the

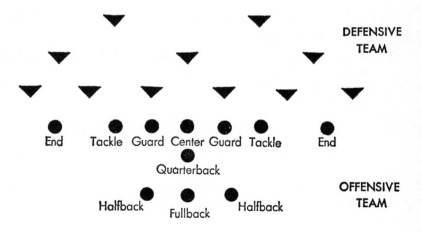

DEFENSIVE
TEAM

End    Tackle  Guard  Center  Guard  Tackle    End

Quarterback

OFFENSIVE
TEAM

Halfback    Fullback    Halfback

defensive men. That is, they can use their hips, shoulders, or arms held against the body.

However, the defensive players are allowed to use their hands for warding off an opponent and for tackling the ball carrier.

This chapter deals with a few of the basic methods used in football for stopping an opponent and for advancing the ball. It should help you observe how scientific principles are put into action.

## Blocking is a big job

Blocking is the hard-hitting work of the players who make a path and keep it open for the man carrying the ball. Most of the blocking is done by the guards and tackles. That is why they are usually the strongest and heaviest players. However, the backfield must also be ready for effective blocking.

When two husky players charge into each other, the one with the greatest momentum will usually continue to move forward. It is therefore up to the blocker to develop as high a speed as he can, as quickly as possible. Since the opposing player is so close, you can see that there is very little time to overcome inertia and gather speed.

One of the things a player does to help himself is to dig his cleats into the ground. This added friction prevents slippage and allows him to exert a stronger force backward. Now the reaction to this force will send him forward. Notice that the stance of the crouching blockers puts him into an excellent position for this "push-off."

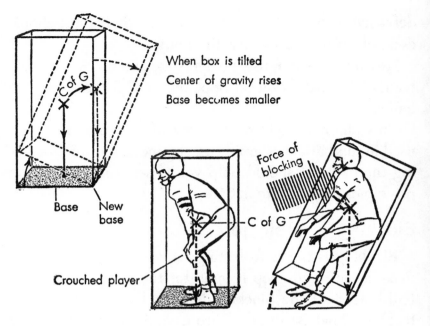

When box is tilted
Center of gravity rises
Base becomes smaller

Force of blocking

C of G

Base    New base

Crouched player

## Blocking is "uplifting" work

A blocker must exert a lifting force on his opponent after the impact. This upsets stability more easily. Let us see why.

Look at the box in the illustration. When the box is resting on one edge, the center of gravity is over the center of the base.

When the box is tilted, see how the center of gravity moves along an arc and is *raised*. But now the stability of the box is less because:

1. the base has become very small.
2. the center of gravity has been raised.
3. the center of gravity is *outside* the base.

For the same reasons, blocking with an upward tilting motion makes it easier to upset an opponent.

Now you can see why blocking is such hard work. The blocker is actually lifting the opposing man. Without the lifting action the opponent may only be shoved backward. He may even keep his stability and remain on his feet.

Of course, if one blocker has much more momentum than his opponent he can upset him, even without any noticeable lifting action.

Keep in mind that the lifting action is not the only movement of the blocker. First, he must go forward from his stance. He acquires most of his momentum during this forward motion.

## Tackling is not tickling!

Tackling is one of the most important actions of the defensive team. It is a heroic attempt to stop the player who is carrying the ball.

There are many reasons why tackling is a man-sized job. One of the biggest difficulties is that the ball carrier is usually one of the fastest runners on the team. It is not easy to catch up with him. Especially when he is preceded by his own men determined to clear a path for him. The tackler is a ready target for these blockers.

The ball carrier also pivots, crosses over, dodges, and side steps. This use of inertia throws his would-be tacklers off balance. It prevents them from choosing the exact moment and location for launching their attacks.

If the tackler has to approach from the side, he does not run straight for the ball carrier. He will not be there when the tackler arrives. The tackler calculates his speed and distance. He runs to a point *ahead* of the runner.

This setting of a "collision course" calls for accurate judgment. If the tackler makes an error in several inches he may be unable to catch his man. The penalty may be a scored touchdown.

## How a player is tackled

A good tackle should be designed to throw the ball carrier down. When a tackle is made high, the runner is only slowed down as he continues to drag the tackler behind him.

An effective tackle is made low so that the knees or legs cannot move. The inertia of the ball carrier makes him continue moving forward. He therefore makes an arc toward the ground. It is similar to tripping a person.

Watch how a tackler starts his tackle from the foot *away* from the carrier. He aims to strike the runner halfway between the knees and hips. He uses the shoulder nearer the runner for the impact. Then he drops his outside shoulder and reaches his arms around behind the runner's legs. He squeezes the knees and legs together.

There are tackles from other positions too, but always the legs and knees are squeezed so that inertia can upset the runner's balance. That is, the center of gravity moves outside the base of the runner.

## How a tackled man falls

When the ball carrier falls he must avoid injury. He must also hold on to the ball and not fumble it.

The advice given to him is to relax completely while hugging the ball. He bends his knees so that he rolls with the fall. This shortens the height that he falls. But it also increases the time for his slowing down. The result is that the impact is lessened.

See how his arms are pulled in. Also watch how he uses his shoulder pads for taking up some of the shock.

## Passing the ball

Some of the most spectacular moments in a football game occur when the ball is passed. This is an excellent method for advancing the ball toward the goal.

There are passes to the side and even to the rear. These have hardly any restriction. On a forward pass, however, there are certain restrictions.

The thrower *must* be behind the line of scrimmage. Also, the ball can be caught only by a teammate who was located at the end of the line, or at least one yard behind the line at the beginning of the play.

These severe restrictions mean that in order for a forward pass to be successfully completed, it must be executed with split-second perfection. Otherwise, the opposition can pounce upon the passer or the receiver.

The receiver must overcome his inertia and start running ahead into enemy territory even before the passer has the ball. Notice how the passer holds the ball with both hands until he is ready to throw the ball. This helps prevent fumbles. He withholds throwing the ball so that his receiver can gain distance. Meanwhile the opposing team may be closing in on him.

91

He gets the proper grip on the ball. Because it takes time for the ball to travel, he aims his trajectory so that he is actually throwing *ahead* of his receiver. Watch how he holds the ball behind his ear and how his other arm is outstretched for balance and for follow-through.

The receiver also has his troubles. The defensive players are running toward him. They will attempt to catch the ball or tackle him the instant that he gets the ball. He must avoid them. His arms are high and stretched toward the ball. He must catch this ball on the run, with his body turned, and perhaps at a slant.

The forward pass has been subject to many rule changes. Today, it is one of the most competitive plays in the game.

## Kicking the ball

Another way to advance the ball toward a team's goal line is to kick it.

A football travels away from the kicker's foot faster than the top of the shoe moves at impact. When the shoe depresses the football, the air inside it gets squeezed. As air particles spring back to their original condition, a force is exerted backward upon the shoe. The reaction causes the ball to go forward.

The ball's forward motion also comes from the momentum it acquires from the kicking foot. As has been said before, the longer the contact of the foot with the ball, the more the ball increases in speed.

That is why a kicker follows through, so that he often looks like a ballet dancer. Very often he may have his foot above his head at the end of a kick. His momentum often picks him off the ground.

There is another reason why the kicker's foot is in contact with the ball longer than you may think. The tip of the shoe touches the ball while the dent in the leather *is being made*. It is still in contact with the ball while the dent *is coming out* of the ball!

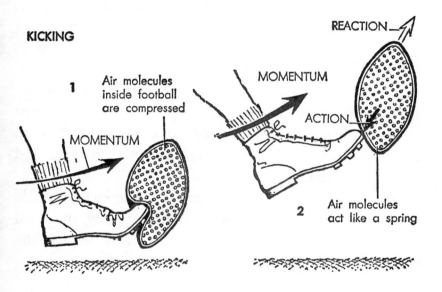

KICKING

1  Air molecules inside football are compressed

MOMENTUM

MOMENTUM

REACTION

ACTION

2  Air molecules act like a spring

## Punts should be hard to catch

A PUNT is a special type of kick made before the ball touches the ground. It is not made with the toe. Instead, the ball is dropped on the top of the foot between the toe and the ankle.

The ball is purposely given a fast spin in order to make it difficult for the opponent to catch. This is done by having the ball point slightly to one side as it is dropped on the foot and kicked.

A punt is most often used on a fourth down when a quarterback sees that his team might not make the necessary 10 yards. He does not wish the opponents to get possession of the ball in a location favorable to them. He therefore orders the ball to be kicked far into enemy territory. A punt is usually aimed so that it will go out of bounds near the opponent's goal line. This prevents a defensive player from running back with the ball.

## Punting on windy days

A good punter uses the wind to help him get distance. If the wind is blowing *toward* the kicker, the ball is sent out with the nose low. This makes the ball move through the air at a low angle. There is less wind resistance and the ball goes far.

On the other hand, if the wind is at the kicker's back, the ball's nose is directed upward more. Now, the wind has more of the ball to blow on. The ball is kept in the air longer and more distance is gained.

## Other kicks

A place kick is made by kicking the ball from a position on the ground. The ball is usually held in place by a teammate. This type is used for scoring field goals and points after a touchdown. It is also used for kickoffs.

A special place kick which is very hard to catch is called a SPINNER. This is made by placing the ball flat on the ground with the ends pointing to the side lines. It does not lift off the ground more than a few feet. When it strikes the ground it bounces in a wild manner.

A team must decide whether it wants a high or a low kickoff. Usually, if a kick is high, it does not go as far as one kicked at a lower angle. However, a high ball takes longer to come down. This prevents the receivers from getting off to a running start. It also allows the kicker's team to get downfield.

If the opposing team has a very good broken-field runner who may receive the ball, the ball may be purposely kicked high.

## Touch football

This popular sport is played in schools and by factory and office workers, both young and old. It is an active and enjoyable game but it is not as rough as regular football.

The reason few injuries occur is that there is no tackling. Instead, the ball carrier is considered stopped when he is tagged by a defensive player. Also, no blocking can be done by a player while his feet are off the ground.

Otherwise, the rules are almost the same as those in regular football.

## Seeing more at a football game

### Why the huddle?

Before almost every play there is a huddle. This is no time for idle conversation or unnecessary discussion, since only twenty-five seconds are allowed for the huddle and for putting the ball into play.

There is a reason why the players form their bodies into a tight circle during a huddle. This helps overcome the noise of the crowd. They can hear each other better.

Here the quarterback listens to any report of an opponent's weakness or strength. He then tells his team the signal for the coming play.

### Changing goals

At the end of the first and third quarters the teams change goals. The ball is replaced exactly the same distance from the goal, but at the other end of the field.

Give yourself some mental exercise by trying to determine exactly where the ball is going to be relocated.

## Surprise kicks

Deception is frequently used in kicking. Everybody expects a punt to be made on the fourth down. But sometimes a team may surprise the opposition with a "quick kick." This may even come during the first or second down.

Then you may see the football sail right over the heads of the entire defensive backfield. They were playing too close to the scrimmage line, not expecting the kick. Inertia kept them from running back fast enough.

Sometimes this strategy is the deciding play in the entire game.

## Kickoff observation

In the early days of football there developed a dangerous and unsportsmanlike evil. The players would place themselves into a tight formation and completely surround their ball carrier.

Then this mass of humanity would run toward the goal. Nothing could stop them. Anyone who tried would be seriously hurt. One of these formations was called the FLYING WEDGE.

Finally the play was outlawed. During a kickoff, you may see how well the rules prevent too many players from gathering around the ball.

There are strict regulations concerning the placement of defensive players at kickoff. Even the offensive players cannot recover the kicked ball unless it has gone at least ten yards.

## Ball carrier's "straight-arm"

Watch how a ball carrier takes advantage of his privilege of using his arms to push away or unbalance a tackler.

A player will say that he is using a "stiff-arm" or a "straight-arm." Actually, his elbow is rarely in a locked position. His arm is slightly bent.

In this way it absorbs the shock against his body as he strikes an opponent. This action is similar to that of springs or shock absorbers under a car. The bowlegged landing gear on airplanes is another good illustration of this shock-absorbing principle. The purpose, as you know, is to allow an impact to be slowed down for a longer time.

If the ball carrier's arm were really stiff, his body would receive the shock of every contact. There would be a stronger possibility of jarring the ball loose from its cradle under the arm. Fumbles are always costly.

## Mixing up the blocks

An interesting observation is to see how a blocker at the scrimmage line tries to use a different type of block at every play.

Since the opponent is usually the same person, it would be poor strategy to always use the same technique. After a while, the opponent would anticipate the next move and prepare himself.

That is why a lineman must use deception and employ an assortment of blocks. You do not have to be an expert to see this. Each block is somewhat different. You can tell when a player mixes them up.

Sometimes two blockers decide to take one defensive player out of action. A 2-on-1 block is extremely effective.

## Watch the gun

When time is almost up and there are only seconds to play, watch the timer's gun. First you will see the puff of smoke. Then you will hear the report of the gun.

The farther away you are sitting, the longer will be the time between the smoke and the sound. This is especially obvious to anyone sitting far away in a big bowl stadium.

Sound travels about ⅕ of a mile in a second. Light travels about 186,000 miles in the same time.

## Public-address system

If the stadium has loud speakers for making announcements you can often hear the same words said several times.

This may not be due only to echoes. You may be sitting at different distances from the various loud-speakers. You hear the sound from a nearby loud-speaker first. Then you hear the same sound again, but from a distant speaker.

## Fantastic research

The next time you see two players running into each other, think of the following facts unearthed by scientists.

Recently some engineers were designing escape cock-pits for faster-than-sound bombers. These cockpits were to be shot away from the plane by explosive charges. The engineers wished to know how much of a speeding-up force a person could take and survive.

They connected their instruments to two football guards. These men then ran toward each other from positions 40 yards apart. One tackled the other head-on to stop him in his tracks. To the utter amazement of everyone, it was discovered that the men repeatedly withstood 70 g's safely. A "g," by the way, is the rate at which gravity speeds up a falling body. It is also commonly referred to as the force which gravity normally exerts on a body.

Actually, the shock only lasted for one-hundredth of a second. But this is about the same time which the bomber crewmen would have to undergo high g forces. So the engineers were able to build their escape mecha-nism.

It is doubtful whether a person could stand this in-crease in speed for any length of time. Even astronauts are not speeded up so quickly during take-offs.

## Gridiron lines

The football field is 360 feet long and 160 feet wide. Each goal line is 30 feet from the end of the field. This leaves 300 feet, or 100 yards, between the goal lines.

The field is usually marked off in lines which are 5 yards apart. The lines are applied either wet or dry. Dry markers use kalsomine, lime, silica powder, or marble dust.

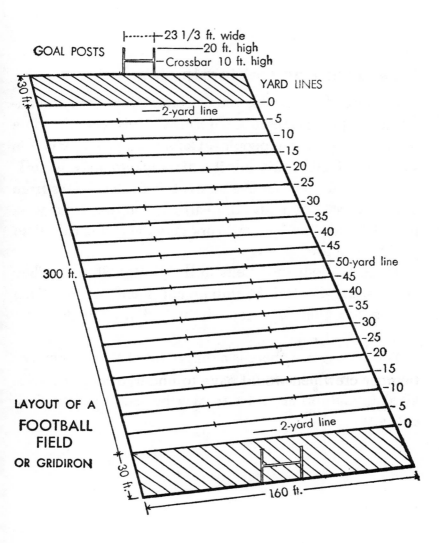

GOAL POSTS

23 1/3 ft. wide
20 ft. high
Crossbar 10 ft. high

30 ft.

YARD LINES

—0
— 5
—10
—15
— 20
—25
—30
—35
— 40
— 45
—50-yard line
—45
—40
— 35
— 30
—25
—20
—15
—10
— 5
—0

2-yard line

300 ft.

LAYOUT OF A
FOOTBALL
FIELD
OR GRIDIRON

2-yard line

30 ft.

160 ft.

The 10 yards, which must be made in four downs are not measured by these lines. Instead, the lineman measures the distance with a 10-yard chain which is attached to two movable metal posts.

See how the lines seem to come together in the distance. This optical illusion is called PERSPECTIVE.

## New York and California time

Because of television, you can sit in New York and enjoy a football game in California. However, the time often confuses some people. Games are often played in sunlight in California while it is already dark in New York.

The sun seems to move across the United States from east to west. Actually, the earth is rotating from west to east. That is why New York gets the sun earlier than the West Coast.

There are four time belts in the United States. They are Eastern, Central, Mountain, and Pacific time. Each belt is one hour later than its neighboring belt to the west.

This means that there is a difference of three hours between New York and California. A football game televised in California at 4 P.M. will be seen in New York at 7 P.M.

# BASKETBALL

## Basketball—a game of speed

Basketball is one of the fastest foot games on earth. Only players who are in topnotch condition can play this strenuous game. There is very little chance to rest while the clock is running.

The game is not like baseball, which gives players a rest when they are not up. Nor is it like football, where a player can catch his breath during the huddle which usually occurs before every play.

During a football game the ball does not change hands many times. In basketball, however, the ball may change hands every ten seconds. Frequently changes occur faster than that.

Under present rules, movement is almost continuous throughout the game. There is very little time for planning. That is why the team must be highly trained and coordinated. Responses to situations must be very quick —almost automatic.

The players put great strain upon their muscles. There is a constant jarring of their bodies; sudden starting, stopping, pivoting, dodging, jumping and running to strategic locations. Players must have agility, endurance, good eyesight, and intelligence.

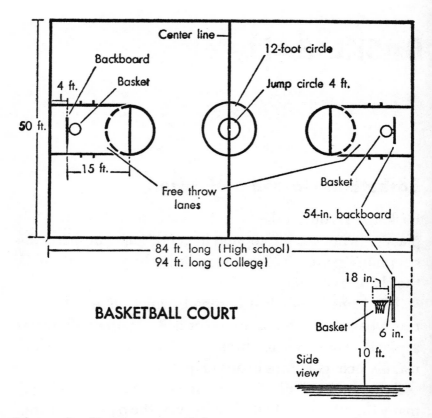

**BASKETBALL COURT**

## Played all over world

Many people believe that the Mayas in Mexico had a game which somewhat resembled basketball. However, in 1891, Dr. James Naismith of Springfield, Massachusetts, devised the game from which our present rules have developed.

He was a physical-education instructor looking for an indoor game to be played between the football and the baseball seasons. That is, from November to late March.

Today hundreds of millions of players and spectators enjoy basketball all over the world. In most countries it is probably the most popular game, next to soccer.

Look around you and you can see baskets everywhere. Find them in playgrounds, backyards, school basements, and on poles and garages.

## Size of courts

The largest court allowed by the rules is 94 feet long and 50 feet wide. This is the size used by colleges and by professionals.

High-school courts are usually about 84 feet long and 50 feet wide. If you see any smaller courts, it is because there is no strict rule for younger players.

The lines on the court are very carefully measured according to regulations.

## How basketball got its name

The first goal was really a peach basket. Later, an iron ring was used with a closed net under it. Someone in the balcony had to take the ball out after each goal. Sometimes a stepladder had to be used.

A person could also push a pole from below and punch the ball out. Years later a net was designed which opened when a referee pulled a string.

To this day the expression "basket" is still used. The white cord net also remains. It extends 15 inches below the rim. This makes it easier to see the ball which is slowed up as it goes through. The net also makes the ball fall down right under the basket.

Today's basket is made of a ⅝ inch-thick iron ring which is 18 inches across. It is usually painted a bright orange color for greater visibility.

The rim is 10 feet above the ground.  The nearest part of the ring is 6 inches away from the backboard.

The basket is 15 feet away from the foul line.

## Why backboard projects into the court

The backboard is a rectangle 6 feet wide and 4 feet high.  Its bottom edge is 9 feet above the floor.  Sometimes you may see fan-shaped backboards.

They are made of wood, steel, or any solid material.  Colleges use backboards made of transparent glass so that spectators sitting behind can see the basket.  Target areas 24 inches by 18 inches are painted on the glass above the basket.

A regulation basket hangs 4 feet inside the end lines.  This gives the players a little room behind it so that they do not go out of bounds easily.

When the game was first invented, the backboards were attached right on the gymnasium walls.  There was no overhang.  The players had a trick of "running up the wall" with their rubber shoes to score.  That is not possible today.

## Why a basketball bounces

In a solid, there is very little space between particles.  It is hard to press it out of shape.

But in a gas there is a great deal of space between particles.  That is why air, which is made up of gases, can be squeezed.

When the basketball strikes the solid floor or backboard it continues to move because of its inertia.  This

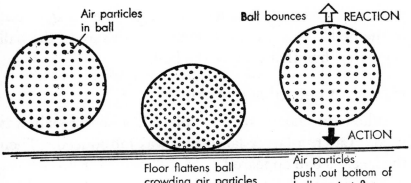

Air particles in ball

Ball bounces ⬆ REACTION

⬇ ACTION

Floor flattens ball crowding air particles

Air particles push out bottom of ball against floor

flattens the ball where it strikes the floor. The particles of air are now squeezed closer through the ball.

The compressed air acts as a spring and pushes the ball back into its round shape. This forces the flat part of the ball against the floor. Reaction pushes the ball away from the floor.

The harder the throw to the floor, the greater is the reaction. That is why the ball bounces faster and higher.

A soft ball is "dead" because there are not enough gas particles in it to cause a springlike action. On the other hand, the air pressure in a basketball can sometimes be too great. Then it becomes very "lively."

Most basketballs are pumped up until the air-pressure gauge reads between 7 and 9 pounds per square inch. This gauge tells only the air pressure *above* the ordinary air pressure all around us, which is about 15 pounds per square inch. A gauge reading of 7 pounds is really 7 plus 15, or 22 pounds per square inch.

If the pressure in the ball were really 7 pounds per square inch, it would be squeezed by the greater outside pressure. Also, when a leak develops, the air goes *out* of the ball. This proves that the air pressure in the ball is greater than that outside the ball.

## How basketballs are made

When the game was first played, a soccer ball was used. Later, a larger laced ball was introduced. Then the laceless ball appeared.

The present-day basketball contains a rubber bladder, carefully covered with rubberized fabric. It is placed in a mold and vulcanized. Then leather sections are cemented to the ball. The entire ball is again placed in a mold and heat-treated.

Whenever air is pumped into a ball it is injected into a self-sealing valve by means of a hollow needle.

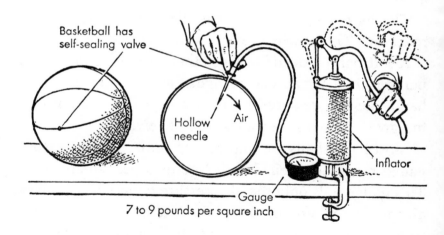

Basketball has self-sealing valve

Hollow needle

Air

Inflator

Gauge

7 to 9 pounds per square inch

The official ball is from 29½ to 30 inches in circumference. It must weigh between 20 to 22 ounces.

Most college and professional games use an orange or

bright tan colored ball.  This makes it highly visible for today's high-speed, fast-breaking game.  Yellow covers are especially good for outdoor twilight play.

## How the ball's bounce is tested

It is important that all basketballs used in tournaments have the same bounce.

First, the ball is inflated to the usual pressure.  Then it is dropped to a solid wooden floor from a height of 6 feet.

Regulations state that the ball must rebound to a height between 49 and 54 inches.

Increasing or decreasing air pressure usually regulates the bounce in a new ball.

## Basketball is a non-contact game

The rules emphasize very clearly that basketball was designed to keep players free from body contacts.

There must be no touching, holding, tripping, charging into an opponent or hacking at his arm.

The penalties for such personal fouls may consist of free basket shots for the opponents, and loss of possession of the ball.  If a player commits fouls consistently, he is sent out of the game.

You will notice that the rules are broken more frequently in basketball than in baseball or even football. The reason is that basketball is a much speedier game. The playing area is much smaller.  Ten players constantly running around are bound to come into contact more often than in the other games.

## How the game is speeded up

More spectators watch basketball than any other game. In order to make it thrilling for them, the rules have been changed to make the game faster.

The game is highly organized. It is often difficult to know all the rules. Remember, however, that each penalty was designed to overcome some evil of the past.

For example, years ago a team that was ahead in the final minutes of play would "freeze" the ball. They would hold onto the ball and not risk a try for further baskets. That is why there is a ten-second rule today. This rule states that a team which has possession of the ball must advance the ball into the opponent's half of the court within ten seconds. The penalty is loss of possession of the ball.

There is also a rule which prevents a player from holding the ball more than five seconds when returning it from out of bounds. And there are other time-limiting rules.

A most important change in the rules was the elimination of the center jump. Formerly, there used to be a center jump after each goal—whether it was a field goal or a successful free throw. Now after a field goal, the opposing team gains possession of the ball and throws it in from out of bounds. This speeds up the game considerably.

Today the game is extremely fast. It is not unusual to witness games scoring over 100 points.

## Moving the basketball

A hush falls over the excited spectators as the referee prepares to throw up the ball for the center jump which starts the game. The two tall opposing players have placed their feet inside the smaller of the two circles in the center of the court. These men are called CENTERS.

The other eight players wait expectantly outside the larger circle, for the ball to be tapped to one of them. As the ball is thrown up, one of the jumpers taps the ball to a teammate—and the game is on!

From now on, each team must move the ball toward its basket according to definite rules. A player cannot run with the ball. In fact, he can take only one step with the same foot in any direction while holding the ball.

However, he can pass the ball to a teammate who is in a more desirable location. He can also advance the ball by bouncing it as he runs alongside, a process called DRIBBLING.

## Passing

Wherever possible, two hands are used for passing. The ball is quite large for most one-handed palm grips. Two hands guide the ball more accurately.

THROWING A BALL
AHEAD OF RUNNER

See how a good player passes the ball to his teammate
—*away* from an opposing player. Also watch how a
player uses inertia to his advantage. Before he passes
the ball, he makes a fake motion in another direction.
His guard moves in this direction. Now, when the pass
is made in a new direction the guard's inertia prevents
him from making a sudden change. He is unable to
block the pass in time.

When catching a pass, the hands give with the thrown
ball. This decreases the impact and prevents the ball
from bouncing out of the hands.

In a tightly guarded position, you may see a player
pass the ball by bouncing it to a teammate. This is
another method of deceiving an opponent by taking
advantage of his inertia. He thinks the ball is going to
be thrown upward, and he cannot change his position
in time.

Players are also instructed not to pass the ball too fast
to a receiver who is running hard *toward* the ball. His
speed adds impact to the catch, and it increases the
danger of fumbling.

However, notice how a ball is thrown to a player running away from the passer. This time the ball is thrown *ahead* of the runner. During the time that the ball is in flight, the runner is also moving forward. The trajectory must be estimated carefully.

Many players receive a pass in a half-crouching position. This saves a split second in getting the ball into a dribble. It is also easier to immediately throw the ball to another player.

Sometimes you will see a hook pass. Here the ball is passed with one hand by holding it in the palm. If time permits, the thrower will bring the ball some distance behind him. In this way he can gather speed for a longer time. He can send the ball far. Watch how his other arm is extended. At the moment when he throws the ball, this front arm moves backward very quickly.

The player is using the principle of reaction to help him. In other words, as the arm goes *backward,* reaction helps drive the ball *forward.*

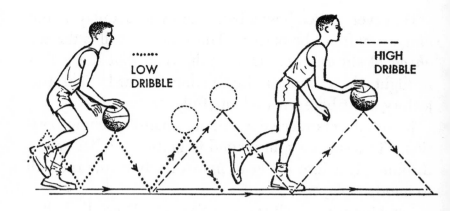

LOW DRIBBLE

HIGH DRIBBLE

## Dribbling

A player who dribbles and stops may not start dribbling again unless the ball is touched by an opponent. He must pass the ball or try for a goal. This rule prevents stalling, and speeds up the game.

Watch the technique of a good dribbler. He does not slap the ball. He pumps the ball mainly by wrist and finger action, and not only with the palm.

A high dribble is very easily stolen by an opponent because of the length of time that it is in the air. Therefore, a high dribble is only used for speed when running. Notice how the ball is bounced hard and with a large forward angle.

Where the defense is very active the ball is dribbled very low. In this way, the ball is in the air for a shorter time. It is under the dribbler's instant control. See how the fingers are kept spread over as wide an area of the ball as possible.

114

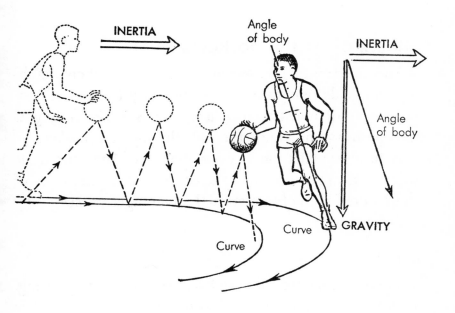

Watch how a good dribbler curves around an opposing player whom he is trying to avoid. See how his body is slanted toward the inside of the curve.

A runner slants his body because inertia is making his body continue to move in a straight line. If he wishes to turn, he must use force to overcome this inertia. When he slants his body he is really "falling" in the opposite direction from where inertia tends to make him move. In this way he is using the force of gravity to help overcome inertia.

He also uses the muscles of his legs to help him turn. He pushes harder against the floor with the foot which is on the outside of the curve. Reaction pushes him away from that direction. You can even hear the uneven footsteps of a runner making fast turns.

# Shooting for the basket

Spectators probably get most enjoyment when watching the goals being made. They enjoy the smooth coordination demonstrated by a player as he skillfully gets into position and sends the ball through the basket.

A brief explanation is given below of the four basic shots. However, many players use combinations of these in order to obtain special advantages possessed by each one.

## Lay-up shot

This is a standard shot used very frequently for scoring. There is much science used in perfecting it.

The player dribbles the ball in fast from either side of the basket. At the best moment, he leaps into the air, holding the ball in his raised hand. He now places the ball against the backboard at a point just above the rim.

Notice how gently the lay-up is made, regardless of the player's approaching momentum. This is the secret of a successful lay-up. There is a good scientific reason why he can do this.

Watch how he releases the ball *at the height of his leap.* This is the point where he no longer has much speed. Most of his momentum was used to overcome gravity when he made his leap. At this moment he can lay the ball exactly where he wants to!

Much practice is necessary to make the coordination automatic. Observe that when a lay-up is made from the right, the player has the ball in his right hand. He

116

leaves the floor with his left foot. Coming in from the left, he has the ball in his left hand. He leaps with his right foot.

Sometimes a lay-up is not made from the right or left. When the dribbler approaches from the middle, he does not use the backboard. He lays the ball over the front of the rim.

## Set shot

This is a try for a goal which is made by a player from a spot quite a distance from the basket.

A player knows the proper trajectory to the basket for any distance. He develops this skill by constant practice.

He must have excellent muscular coordination as well as keen eyesight.

It is exciting to see an expert sink most of his set shots into the basket. Some can make spectacular shots from the mid-court line—and farther! During one college game an 85-foot set shot was successfully completed.

Long shots need higher trajectories. If your gymnasium has a low ceiling you will find that a player cannot try extremely distant set shots.

Many players use two hands for set shots. In recent years, more and more of these shots are being made with only one hand. Some coaches feel that with one hand,

HOOK
SHOT

JUMP
SHOT

there are fewer muscles used which can upset one's aim.

Watch carefully and you will see that actually two hands are used when starting a one-handed set shot. One hand holds the ball from below. The other is in the back. It is only the back hand which pushes the ball toward the basket.

## Jump shot

This is the most frequently used shot made close to the basket, especially when the area is crowded. It is made by holding the ball in one hand high above the head, and jumping as high as possible.

At the height of his leap the player turns to the basket. He takes deliberate aim and sends the ball along a small trajectory through the rim. This shot is usually successful because it is not easy for an opponent to block.

## Hook shot

This is another shot which is difficult for an opponent to stop. Strangely enough, it is made when the player is unable to aim. Only practice can teach a player how much push to give the ball.

It is made from either side of the basket. At the start, the player's back is to the basket. The ball is in the player's extended hand. As he runs by the basket he throws the ball over his head to the proper spot on the backboard.

## Sudden changes fool opponents

Watch a player with the ball. He is usually closely

guarded by an opponent. Suddenly he throws the ball in a certain direction. The guard is too slow to prevent this from happening.

This type of evasive action depends upon inertia with which you are already quite familiar. But it also depends upon the fact that everybody has a certain REACTION TIME. This is the time it takes for a person to make a move after he recognizes the need to do so.

When the player throws the ball, or starts to throw the ball, his opponent sees this action. His brain has to interpret what this means. It then sends an electrical signal to his legs and body muscles to follow the first player's movement. It takes a fraction of a second for all this to happen.

By the time he reacts to the throwing of the ball it is too late to do anything about it.

## Faking in basketball

In almost every action a player fakes a movement. He pretends that he is going to do one thing, then he suddenly does something different.

This is called FEINTING. It is designed to throw the opposition off balance. As you learned, it depends upon reaction time and inertia. This device is such a successful one because basketball is an extremely fast game which depends upon split-second reactions.

Watch how a player fakes a set shot. Then suddenly he starts dribbling toward the basket for a lay-up shot. This is done to draw the defense away from the basket for an instant.

Strategy is all important. Very often a team fakes much action in one section of the court, while all the time one player is getting ready to bolt into a position near the basket. He will receive the ball and score in the twinkling of an eye.

## Free throws are gifts

A free throw is the privilege given a player to score one point by an unhindered throw from the foul line. This line is 15 feet from the basket. Originally it was 20 feet.

Years ago every team had one player who specialized in foul shots. Today, the free throws for personal fouls must be made by the person who is fouled. However, if the foul is not a personal foul any member of the team can make the free throw. That is why every player is expected to be an expert free-throw shooter. Authorities agree that a player should be able to make seven or eight successful attempts in ten shots.

In order to become an expert in these not-to-be-missed shots, a player practices constantly. He probably throws about 100 shots a day during a training period. Over one dozen are thrown before every game.

Most free throws are aimed an inch or two above the front rim of the basket. Coaches feel that from a front position it is not easy to get the ball into the basket by striking the backboard first.

Many coaches have the players practice free throws while using smaller baskets. They feel that this sharpens a player's aim.

## More about basketball

### Basketball shoes are "4-wheel brakes"

See how a player's shoes enable him to make those sudden stops, starts, and turns. With the rubber or composition soles, he can hug the smooth wooden floor and "stop on a dime."

In addition to using friction, the soles also hug the floor because of air pressure. Notice the design on the soles. The ridges enclose pockets containing air.

When the player runs or stamps his foot he presses hard on the sole and some of the air is squeezed from these spaces. When he is not pressing hard, or when he begins to lift a foot, the air pressure is lessened in each enclosed part of the sole's design.

The normal air pressure now presses the shoe down to the floor, because it is greater than the air pressure under the design.

Of course, the spaces are made in a special way. A very good vacuum under a basketball shoe is not very desirable. Can you imagine a player helplessly glued to the floor by air pressure!

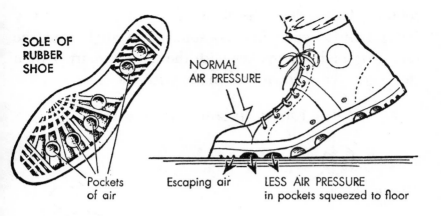

SOLE OF RUBBER SHOE

Pockets of air

NORMAL AIR PRESSURE

Escaping air

LESS AIR PRESSURE in pockets squeezed to floor

## Using "English" on the ball

A player will often give the ball a hard spin as he throws it to the floor or to the backboard. He does this with his wrist and fingers.

He is putting "English" on the ball. This allows him to control the angle at which the ball will bounce. (See illustration.)

Notice how a ball which is not spinning strikes the floor. The angle at which the ball hits is the same angle

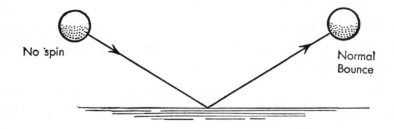

No spin

Normal Bounce

with which the ball bounces away.

What happens when the ball is thrown so that the top of the ball is made to spin *away* from the player? As the rotating ball strikes the floor, the ball bounces away faster than when it had no spin. The angle that the bouncing ball now makes with the floor is sharper than the angle the thrown ball made with the floor.

PUTTING "ENGLISH" ON THE BALL

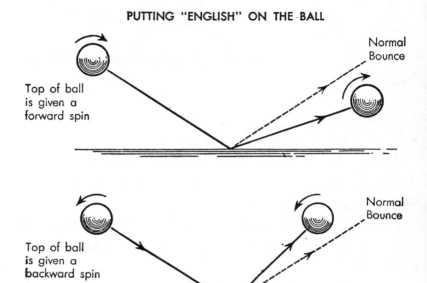

On the other hand, the ball may be thrown to the floor so that the top of the ball is spinning *toward* the player. As the ball bounces, it makes a larger angle with the floor than the thrown ball did.

When throwing the ball at the backboard from one side, the player can put the right kind of English on the ball by spinning it sideways.

Controlling bouncing angles is valuable when the player is shooting from under the basket. A player usually delivers a two-handed shot to the basket so that his palms are turned toward the basket. This wrist motion makes the top of the ball rotate toward the thrower.

When the ball hits the backboard it is slowed up slightly. This causes it to rebound so it is closer to the basket rim.

One of the passes used in tight spots is rolling the ball to a teammate. Here, the top of the ball is made to spin away from the thrower. In this way the ball is not slowed up as it strikes the floor.

## How high is a guard?

Watch a player when he is in a guarding position. Suppose he were to put his hands up in the air as far as he could. How high a barrier would he be making for the player with the ball?

You can find out how much a player's reach adds to his total length. Measure your length with your arms at your side. Now raise your arms high. Measure from the floor to your fingertips.

Most people can stretch above their heads for a distance which is about one-fourth of their height. In other words, suppose a player is 6 feet tall. One-fourth of 72 inches is 18 inches. His fingertips are now 90 inches (72 + 18) above the floor.

Now, suppose he can jump about 30 inches off the floor if necessary. That would make him 120 inches or 10 feet tall!

No wonder a player has to fake in order to get a ball past a guard. He can rarely throw it over or through him!

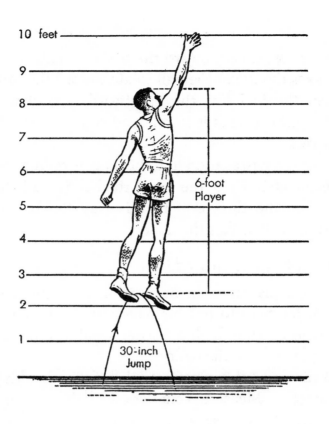

10 feet

9

8

7

6

5

4

3

2

1

6-foot
Player

30-inch
Jump

## Those tall players

Every year basketball players get taller and taller.
Today's average height is approaching 6 feet, 5 inches.
Some men are gigantic. Wilt Chamberlain, for example,
is 7 feet, 1 inch.

Many people say that to make the game competitive,
there should be an attempt made to match teams of
approximate heights. Some years ago the Olympic
games limited the height of players. However, such a
fuss was raised that this ruling was removed.

The elimination of the frequent center jump (it is

still used a few times in the game) helped matters somewhat. But in the main, little has been done about the problem of unmatched teams.

You have learned that a 6-foot player can easily reach 10 feet when he jumps and stretches. The basket rim is only 10 feet above the floor! Can you see what an advantage a 6½-foot player possesses?

See how easily the jump shots and lay-ups are made by the lanky players. Taking rebounds is often like child's play.

People are getting taller in our country. Better diets, especially while growing up, are probably most responsible for this. General improved health of our nation is important too. Heredity, of course, plays a very important part in bringing taller people into the world.

Remember too, that there were always tall men in our population. They just were not trained to become basketball champions as they are today. Now tall athletes are usually selected and advised to go into basketball.

## Players cannot go on forever

You may think that the players keep running around continuously. It makes you tired just to look at them panting and sweating.

Watch them carefully. You will discover that there are many moments when they rest and catch their breath. There are intervals between halves, frequent time-outs, substitutions, free throws, and many other stopping places.

Without these, the players would be in a complete

state of collapse at the end of the game. Keep records of these "rest periods." You will be surprised how they add up.

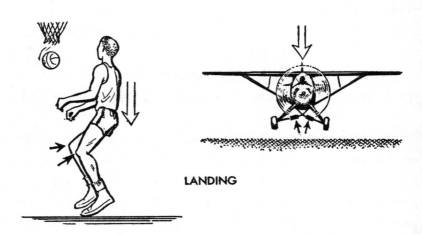

LANDING

## Athletes land gently

Players must prevent hurting their muscles. Observe all the little tricks they use.

When landing from a jump, a player will come down with his knees bent. This takes up the shock by making the slowing-down force act for a longer time and distance. The landing gear on an airplane has shock absorbers which work on the same principle.

See how a player follows through, falls loosely, pulls a ball back when catching it, swings his arms. Coordination is the secret for preventing strained muscles.

Constant practice and training have taught him how to protect his body. An untrained player has sore muscles for many days after a strenuous game. An athlete who is in condition can keep going every day.

## Why gymnasiums are noisy

The walls of gymnasiums are usually made of a stone-like material called TILE. This hard surface reflects sound very easily.

People cheer, scream, whistle, or make other shrill sounds. These bounce off the tile and back to your ears. But you are not really hearing echoes most of the time.

Your ears can hear two sounds only if the sounds are at least one-tenth of a second apart. Sound travels 1,120 feet per second, or 112 feet in one-tenth of a second. Therefore, to produce an echo that you can detect, sound has to travel at least 112 feet. To cover that round-trip distance, the wall must be 56 feet away from you.

Usually you are closer than that to a wall. So you cannot be hearing an echo. Instead, you are getting a series of very short and quick sound reflections called REVERBERATIONS (ree-verb-er-AY-shonz).

As each sound returns to your ear, it merges with the sound you heard a moment before. This build-up makes the sound *louder*.

When mats are hung on the walls the sound is lessened. Also, when there are many people in the gym they too absorb sound vibrations. They also prevent sound from reaching the hard walls.

Many gymnasiums use sound-absorbing materials for the ceiling and upper walls. You will notice the difference in noise level immediately. Look for these special tiles. They are made of soft material and may have many tiny holes in them.

## About the athlete's body

The body is a complicated machine. It is capable of performing the most delicate skills in sports calling for the utmost muscular control. But, whenever necessary, the body can also use powerful muscles for extremely strenuous activities.

People often ask doctors whether engaging in sports is harmful. Are not certain sports too strenuous? Cannot the heart and other organs be permanently damaged?

The general opinion of physicians is that the body is built to withstand tremendous strains for a while. In fact, it is good to exercise. But all doctors warn that first a person must be given a very careful examination. This is to make sure that the body can stand the necessary exertion.

Every good athlete takes the time to learn about his body, and how to care for it. He develops good health habits and proper techniques in his sport. These help prevent injury and improve his performance.

## The heart is a pump

The heart is a remarkable organ which pumps blood to the lungs and through the body.

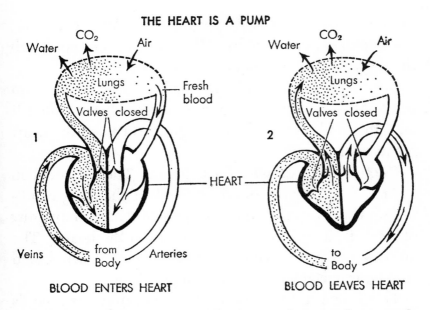

THE HEART IS A PUMP

BLOOD ENTERS HEART          BLOOD LEAVES HEART

In the lungs the blood comes very close to the outside air. Here it picks up fresh oxygen. It also gets rid of wastes, such as carbon dioxide and water vapor. As the blood goes through the lungs, it also gives off some of the heat which is produced by the body. You can feel this heat by "huffing" on your hands.

During exercise the athlete's heart beats faster because it has a bigger job to do. The muscle cells need more oxygen. They are also producing more waste products and heat.

The normal heart beat is about sixty-five to seventy times a minute. Research scientists have recorded the heart beats of athletes playing basketball, tennis, football, and other fast sports.

They find that the average heart beats of these players is 160 per minute! Some slower sports have lower rates, between 126 to 152 beats per minute. After the work, the rate dies down rapidly. However, it does not reach the prework rate for about one-half hour.

For many years people believed that the heart of an active athlete always became enlarged. They called it an "athlete's heart." They thought this ruined the heart for normal living.

Doctors disagree with these ideas. They say that in the main, the heart can adjust itself to changing conditions. However, they do warn people that as they grow older, it is dangerous to put a strain on the heart. The arteries undergo certain changes which lessen blood supply, especially to the heart muscles.

This is one of the reasons why you rarely see records being broken by athletes who are "on in years."

## How muscles work

Did you ever see a skeleton in a doctor's office or in a biology laboratory? Did you notice the wires and pipes holding it up? Without the wires the skeleton would collapse.

Our bones have joints and ligaments connecting the joints. But without muscles supporting the bones, we too would collapse.

There are over 600 muscles in the body. Each muscle consists of bundles of muscle fibers. There may be a million of these fibers in one large muscle. When activated by an electrical nerve signal from the brain, the entire muscle shortens.

No single muscle can move any part of the body in more

than one direction. It must have another muscle to work against it. Look at the illustration of the upper arm.

To bring the lower arm up, the biceps shortens and the triceps relaxes and gets longer. To lower the arm again, the biceps relaxes and gets longer. At the same time the triceps gets shorter.

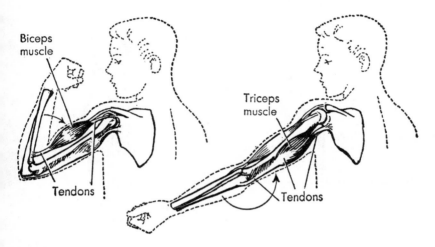

Biceps muscle

Tendons

Triceps muscle

Tendons

It should be clear that the biceps pulls the arm up, and the triceps pulls the arm back. A muscle relaxes only to allow the opposing muscle to do its job.

When a muscle contracts ( gets shorter) it thickens and bunches up. You can feel this bulge when you flex your arm and say, "Feel my muscle."

## Muscles and athletes

Muscles are not attached directly to the bones. A muscle ends in a tendon (see illustration) which is attached to the bone. When an athlete pulls a tendon, this is what he injures.

When the same muscle is exercised day after day, it will increase in size as new cells grow. Not all athletes desire large overdeveloped muscles. A weight lifter's muscles would not be of much use on a basketball court.

In addition to strong muscles, athletes try to build muscles which react quickly. They also want muscles

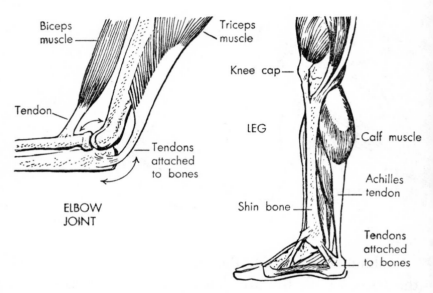

which work smoothly with other muscles. This is called COORDINATION (coh-or-din-AY-shun).

Much coordination is needed to develop a skill in any sport. A great many muscles are used in every movement. For example, there are 150 pairs of muscles involved just in walking!

Can you imagine the coordination needed to be a switch hitter in baseball? Such a player can bat right-handed or left-handed. He is called AMBIDEXTROUS (am-bee-DECK-strus).

Muscle tissue remains in a slight condition of contraction all the time. This condition is called muscle tone. All athletes have good muscle tone.

When a muscle gets tired it must be given a certain time to rest. During this time the blood brings oxygen to it. The blood also removes the waste products formed by the chemical reactions in the muscle cells. A muscle which is not given enough "recovery time" will feel tired.

A "Charley horse" is an injury to a muscle, usually in the leg. A sudden strain can tear some of the fiber bundles, causing pain and swelling. This is a common injury, especially during training periods.

## Breathing

An athlete's normal breathing rate is about sixteen times a minute. But when he has just run a race, or done other strenuous work, he has to breathe more often.

A gasoline engine must have air to operate. If the air is not fed into the cylinders every moment, the gasoline will not ignite.

Strangely enough, the cells in the body behave differently. They are able to continue their complicated chemical work for a while *without* oxygen. That is why a 100-yard-dash sprinter often runs the entire race without taking a single breath! Actually, a sprinter finds that breathing interferes with the extremely fast movements of his arms and legs.

However, when the race is over, the athlete has to pay

back to his body the oxygen which he should have breathed in before. This takes a little time. So the next time you see an athlete's chest and abdomen moving very rapidly, remember—he is paying back his "oxygen debt"!

When an automobile goes fast, its engine needs more oxygen than at normal speeds. In fact, at extremely high speeds the air is pumped into the carburetor of a racing automobile with a "supercharger."

In the same way, an athlete doing heavy work may need as much as fifteen times more oxygen than normally.

Here is another odd fact. It is not so much the lack of oxygen which makes the athlete breathe so heavily. It is rather the build-up of carbon dioxide in his blood. This controls the breathing center in the brain.

## "Second wind"

Sometimes a distance runner, swimmer, or rower may become very uncomfortable after a race is started. The extreme exertion may leave him almost out of breath. His face becomes drawn and worried. Pain may grip his side or his chest. His head often throbs or he gets dizzy.

Suddenly the athelete gets his "second wind" and experiences a feeling of great relief. Breathing becomes deeper and regular and the muscles seem to receive renewed strength. The person feels that he can now go on indefinitely.

The reason for this extraordinary happening is still not completely understood by the medical profession.

It is a highly complicated affair involving many organs and glands of the body.

Doctors believe that when the athlete first starts his strenuous muscular activity, all the parts of his body are not working together. Adjustments must be made in the way bigger amounts of oxygen are taken in and more waste products are eliminated. The heart and blood vessels have to undergo changes to meet the severe demands. Certain chemicals must be poured into the blood to help it do the proper job.

It takes a little time until all the parts start working as a team to supply the needs of the fast-moving muscles. When all adjustments and corrections are made, the athlete gets his "second wind."

Not every runner or swimmer is aware of this sensation. Most highly trained athletes rarely go through it. On the other hand, in some people no adequate adjustment is ever made. These people just have to slow down, quit, or collapse.

## Bones

The 206 bones of the body support and give form to the body. They also protect delicate organs. And they supply a place for attaching muscles.

There are more than 100 joints. Some are merely hinge joints. Others fit together so that one bone can turn inside another. These are called BALL and SOCKET joints. A good example of this type is the shoulder joint. There are many other types of joints.

All movable joints are surrounded by protective cover-

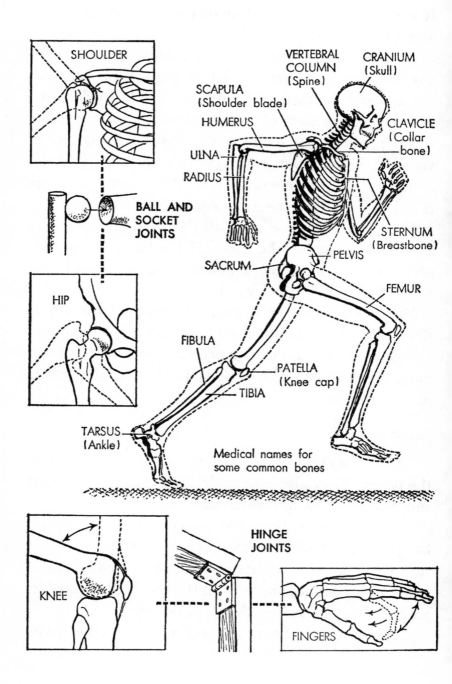

SHOULDER

VERTEBRAL COLUMN (Spine)

CRANIUM (Skull)

SCAPULA (Shoulder blade)

HUMERUS

CLAVICLE (Collar bone)

ULNA

RADIUS

BALL AND SOCKET JOINTS

STERNUM (Breastbone)

HIP

SACRUM

PELVIS

FEMUR

FIBULA

PATELLA (Knee cap)

TIBIA

TARSUS (Ankle)

Medical names for some common bones

KNEE

HINGE JOINTS

FINGERS

ings. Inside these, the joints are well lubricated by special liquids. One of these coverings or sacs is called a BURSA. When a joint gets inflamed, the condition is often called BURSITIS (burr-SITE-iss).

When an athlete uses one particular joint a great deal, it frequently becomes inflamed. The surrounding membrane may then give off more lubricating liquid, and swelling and puffiness result.

These painful joints are commonly called BASEBALL ARM, TENNIS ARM, and WATER ON THE KNEE.

Ligaments hold joints together. They do not stretch easily and frequently tear when they are moved too far. The result is a sprain.

When a bone is forced out of its proper position in a joint, it is called a DISLOCATION. This is a common injury on the football field.

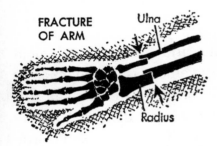

FRACTURE OF ARM — Ulna — Radius

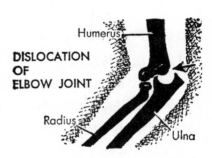

DISLOCATION OF ELBOW JOINT — Humerus — Radius — Ulna

Bones are very strong in certain directions. A thigh bone can be subjected to a pressure of perhaps 20,000 pounds per square inch without breaking. This pressure, however, must be applied from each long end. That is the way this bone supports the body.

But if the same bone receives a blow from the side, it may fracture. Only a few hundred pounds pressure will cause the break.

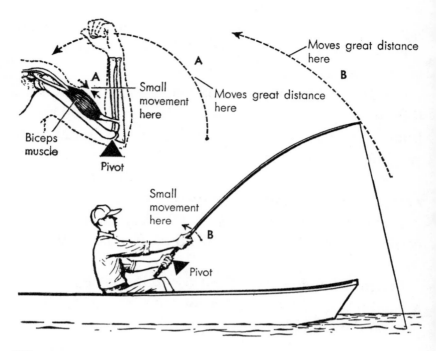

## The arm is a lever

Look at the diagram of the arm. This arrangement makes the arm a lever, with the elbow as the pivot. You can easily see that when the biceps moves a small distance, the hand moves a much greater distance.

A fishing rod is a similar type of lever. (See illustration.) The long pole enables you to apply a force for a small distance near one end of the pole. At the same time, the hook end of the pole is made to move over a much greater distance.

One of the laws of nature is that you must pay for this increase in distance. That is why the force applied by the biceps is *greater* than the force exerted by the hands.

# Control of body temperature

During continuous violent exercise there is much heat produced in the athlete's body. This heat comes mainly from the chemical action in the muscle cells. A person's temperature may actually increase about 1 degree Fahrenheit.

About seven-eighths of this excess heat escapes through the skin, mainly by evaporation. The body has about 2 million sweat glands. Sweat is 99% water. It takes heat to evaporate water. As the sweat evaporates, it takes the heat it needs from the tiny blood vessels near it. This cools the blood.

Football players may lose from 5 to 10 pounds of body weight in a full game. This is mainly due to a loss of water by sweating.

When a player is unable to lose heat normally, the temperature rises. Heatstroke, also called SUNSTROKE, is the result. The skin is hot and dry, the pulse fast, the blood pressure high. The body temperature may rise to 110 degrees Fahrenheit. At this temperature brain cells are destroyed.

Heatstroke is a dangerous condition. Ice packs or cold water are used to get the temperature down quickly.

Athletes subjected to high temperatures and much sweating often get a condition called HEAT EXHAUSTION. Here, strangely enough, the pulse is weak, the skin moist and clammy, the blood pressure low. The person suffering from heat exhaustion should be kept warm and quiet.

During very hot days an active athlete may develop

141

heat cramps in a muscle which is being used most. It has been found that eating salt tablets will safeguard a person against heat cramps.

## What are black and blue marks?

Sometimes a player receives a blow which does not break the skin. After a little while, a purple color may be seen under the skin.

This is caused by blood which escapes from tiny blood vessels called capillaries. When these break because of a blow, the blood flows into the surrounding skin. A "black eye" is produced this way too.

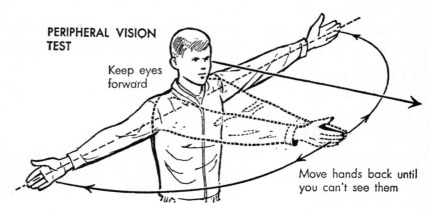

PERIPHERAL VISION TEST

Keep eyes forward

Move hands back until you can't see them

## Side vision

It is very useful in most sports to be able to see sideways while looking straight ahead. This is called PE-RIPHERAL (purr-IF-er-ull) VISION. It enables a player to see an opponent at his side without turning his head.

Test your own peripheral-vision angle. Hold both your hands together at some distance in front of your face. Continue looking straight ahead, and move each hand toward your sides, shoulder high.

You should be able to see both hands, while looking directly ahead, until they are in a straight line. This is 180 degrees. You may even see through an arc of 190 degrees.

## Athlete's foot

This skin infection is caused by a FUNGUS (FUN-gus), which usually attacks the skin between the toes, causing itching, oozing, and wounds which are difficult to heal.

The fungus is picked up from locker-room floors and in showers. Some places have antiseptic foot baths. These will not cure the infection. They only prevent the spread. It is good to wear sandals where other people walk barefooted.

This mold infection may often be checked by wearing clean white stockings. Keep feet dry by sprinkling powder between the toes.

## Knockouts in sports

There are many ways in which a player may receive a blow on the head and black out. In baseball, he may be hit by a pitched ball or collide with another player. Football players may be knocked out when tackled or blocked.

Why does a person become unconscious? First, there is the knockout punch in boxing. A blow is hit "on the button" on the point or side of the chin. This shock is relayed to the back of the skull. Certain important nerves are jolted.

These nerves control the blood pressure to the brain. For one brief instant the brain receives very little blood and the oxygen in it. The brain cannot stand being without a blood supply, even for an instant. Unconsciousness is the result.

Another common type of blackout occurs when the head is jolted in a fall or collision, or is struck by a fast baseball or soccerball. This kind of brain shake-up is called a CONCUSSION.

When the head is made to start or stop suddenly, inertia causes the soft material in the brain to move backward or forward.

There is a certain part of the brain which keeps us conscious and alert. It also has the job of awakening us from sleep. When inertia squeezes this section together —even for a split-second—the player becomes unconscious.

## Science in other sports

You have learned how an understanding of scientific principles can help you become a better player of baseball, football, and basketball. You can also get great enjoyment from many sports if you are aware of the science involved.

In this chapter you will read about sports you engage in very often. You will see that even simple actions are covered by scientific laws.

## Why does a golf ball have dimples?

Believe it or not, the golf balls of over 100 years ago were made of leather, tightly stuffed with goose feathers. After much experimentation, the modern ball was developed.

This has a rubber center, tightly wound with stretched rubber thread. The cover is made of tough composition. The finished ball weighs 1.62 ounces.

At first the balls were smooth. But soon many players observed that old, pitted balls traveled farther and truer. After a while, everybody marked up the new balls before using them. Finally, the golf ball manufacturers placed the dimples on all the balls.

When a smooth golf ball is struck, it makes a nose dive to the earth after a very short distance of about 30 yards. A dimpled ball struck in the same manner, sails straight out in a rising flight. It may land about 230 yards down the fairway.

The strange flight of the smooth ball is explained as follows: As the ball moves forward it pushes the air ahead of it. It is followed by a space with a lessened amount of air in it.

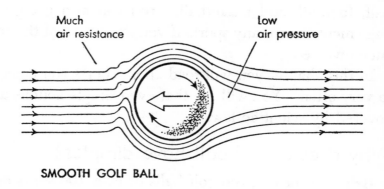

SMOOTH GOLF BALL

There is now a difference in air pressure around the ball; high in front, low in back. This causes a suction-like action which stops the ball and it drops.

You should know, too, that all golf balls are given a backward spin by the golf clubs. This spin may be about 5,000 revolutions per minute.

As the dimpled ball is sent spinning into flight, the little air pockets in it carry air to the rear of the ball.

This prevents the formation of a space with reduced air pressure.

Now the air pressure on the back of the ball is almost as great as it is in front. The dimpled ball sails farther, with less air resistance and with greater accuracy.

Another interesting fact is that a struck golf ball is in contact with the club for only ½,₅₀₀ of a second. Yet in that short time, the ball attains an average speed of 150 miles per hour. This is faster than the club itself is moving on impact.

The extra velocity comes from the fact that the golf

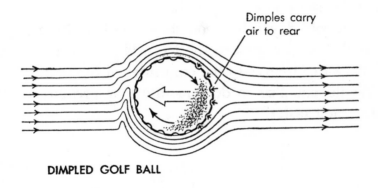

Dimples carry
air to rear

DIMPLED GOLF BALL

ball is squeezed by the impact of the club. As the elastic ball recovers its shape, it presses back against the club. This backward force causes a forward reaction. This motion is added to the motion of the swinging club.

## Why can't we ice-skate on glass?

Many people think that we are able to skate on ice because it is smooth. Why, then, can we not skate on glass or polished granite? These are just as smooth as ice.

People have tried it. Even though the steel runners look smooth, they still scratch the glass. The friction prevents the runners from gliding over the surface.

You can skate on ice because the pressure of the runner causes some of the ice under it to melt. This small film of water has the same function as an oil lubricant, and the skate glides over it.

When the skater passes, the water immediately freezes again. In some extremely cold places in the world, the pressure of the runners is not enough to melt the ice. Then ice skating is not possible.

On a cold day, when you stand too long in one spot, your skates may stick to the ice. This is because some of the water freezes to the cold sides of the skates.

Would you like to demonstrate that pressure causes ice to melt faster?

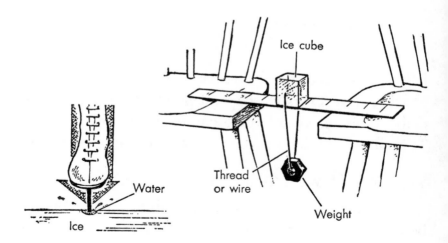

Ice cube

Water

Ice

Thread or wire

Weight

Place a ruler or a flat stick between two chairs. Put an ice cube in the middle of the ruler.

Now lay a length of strong sewing thread or some thin wire across the middle of the ice cube. Tie the ends of the string into a loop. Suspend a heavy weight from the bottom of the loop.

In a short time the pressure of the thread will cause the ice to melt and to refreeze around the string. The string may pass completely through the ice.

## Riding a bicycle

One of the reasons a rider can balance himself on a bicycle is that the wheels are turning. Prove this by trying to balance yourself on a motionless bicycle. It cannot be done for any length of time.

As you learned in the discussion of a spinning football on page 84, a rotating object tends to hold its same spinning position. It resists a change. Scientists call it a gyroscopic effect.

This kind of inertia of a rotating object allows the rider to balance a moving bicycle easily. But it must be emphasized—it is not the forward motion that is needed. It is the turning wheels.

You can show this by tying the wheels to the frame so that they cannot turn. Then balance the bicycle on a slippery, wet surface and push the bicycle forward. You will see immediately that there is no gyroscopic action at work to keep the bicycle erect.

Balance on a bicycle is also maintained by inertia. Suppose the cyclist starts to fall to the right. He im-

ertia makes him continue in a straight line, which is to
mediately turns the front wheel to the right. But in-
the *left* of where he was beginning to fall. This opposite movement straightens him out and makes the bicycle
erect again.

Learning to ride a bicycle is learning how to make the
above adjusting movements unconsciously.


## Movement of arms while running

Try to run while your hands are tied or while you are
holding something with two hands. You certainly are
not going to break any speed records this way.

In fact, this condition is so awkward, you cannot keep
it up long. Your body twists so violently, it hurts.

Let us analyze the reasons for the twist. You know
that every action has a reaction in the opposite direction.
As a leg goes forward, then the rest of the body must react
backward.

Suppose the right leg goes forward. Then the rest of
your right side reacts backward. At the same moment,
the left leg is moving backward. The reaction of your
left side is now forward.

This is the cause of the right and left twist in your
body as one leg and then the other leg is brought forward.

The arms, too, cause body reactions just as the legs
do. As the right arm moves forward, the right side
reacts backward.

Now you can understand how most of the awkward
body twist is removed. The arms and legs on the same
side do not move in the same direction at the same time.

Their opposite reactions on the body lessen the twist.

When we walk or run, the right leg goes forward as the right arm goes backward. You can see this clearly when watching a runner or a hurdler. Athletes use their arms for getting a smoother stride.

## Swimming

In swimming, you make use of the inertia of the water by pushing yourself backward quickly with your arms and legs. If you try to do this very slowly you will find that it is possible to overcome the water's inertia.

When you do not give water enough time to move out of the way, it can behave like a hard surface. A fast slap on the water can actually hurt you. Many a high diver has learned the danger of hitting the water in a flat position.

The other scientific principle which is very important in swimming is reaction. In the water it is very easy to see this in operation. Every action causes a very obvious opposite reaction.

As the water is pushed backward by the arms and legs, the body moves forward. If the swimmer wishes to go upward, he pushes the water downward. He uses this motion if he needs some support or if he wishes to return to the surface.

A swimmer also uses reaction for going downward. He may do this by pushing the water upward.

These motions do not occur because the water is being squeezed or pressed. It is almost impossible to compress water. Swimming movements are due to reactions.

## Momentum in running broad jump

At a track meet, you can watch a broadjumper in action. He runs to the jump-off spot as fast as he can. Then, with the aid of a jump, he lets his momentum carry him through the air. A champion may jump over 26½ feet.

While he is jumping, he may perform certain "walking in the air" movements. You will often hear unscientific people say that these motions help carry the jumper farther.

These folks are greatly misinformed. It should be obvious that it is not possible to increase one's momentum after losing contact with the ground. Unless, of course, one falls from an airplane! Then the force of gravity will speed up the body.

A jumper cannot use a force to increase his speed forward in mid-air. If he has nothing solid to push back upon, then reaction cannot drive him forward.

Any walking motion or other movements while in the air, are to give the jumper balance. It also helps him extend his feet in order to get extra distance. Reaction on his own body prevents him from falling back into a sitting position. Watch how he swings his arms downward and backward.

## High-jumping trajectories

Good high jumpers must use science to their advantage. How else can some of them sail over bars set at over 7¼ feet?

Watch a jumper pace off the number of steps he will use in his run-in. He always starts counting from a spot close to the bar and ends his pacing at his starting point. He does this very carefully.

When he jumps, he wants to be *directly over the bar* when he reaches the highest point in his trajectory. Since this curved "flight path" is very short, any miscalculation of his jumping-off place can mean a loss of height.

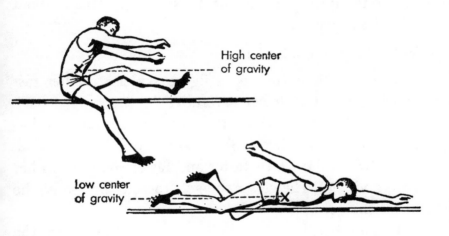

High center of gravity

Low center of gravity

When the jumper is going over the bar he must consider his center of gravity. When clearing the bar, he wishes to raise his center of gravity the shortest possible distance from the bar.

If the scissors style is used, the center of gravity is perhaps 6 inches above the bar. But when the jumper goes over face down, horizontally, his center of gravity is lower. That is why this style is so popular.

## What is a bowling ball made of?

Bowling balls are made of hard rubber. They are 9 inches in diameter. The heaviest weigh up to 16 pounds.

The popular lightweight bowling balls are from 10 to 15 pounds. They have a surface of hard rubber, but inside there is a mixture of rubber and cork.

## Speed of a bowling ball

The average time for a ball to travel from the foul line to the head pin is about 2½ seconds. This is about 25 miles per hour.

## Whirling ice skater

The next time you see a figure skater start her fast whirling act, watch her carefully.

When she starts whirling slowly on one foot, she has her arms outstretched. She also has one leg extended.

But when she whirls faster and faster she pulls in her arms and leg. The closer she gets these to her body, the faster she goes.

It is a scientific principle that to whirl the fastest, the greatest amount of body weight must be as close to the spinning axis as possible.

## Gravity and sports records

Here is an intriguing idea to think about.

The closer one is to the center of the earth, the greater is the pull of gravity. On the other hand, the pull becomes less as one gets farther away from the earth's center.

The equator is about 13 miles farther away from the center of the earth than the North Pole is from the center. Therefore the pull of gravity is less at the equator.

In most sports the championships and world's records often depend upon fractions of an inch. Now, if the pull of gravity is less, then an athlete can jump higher, or throw things farther. *Any champion can break his record by competing in a city closer to the equator.*

Research scientists have calculated that a broadjumper would jump ⅜ inch farther in Texas than he would in Massachusetts.

An Olympic shot-put record set in Finland would be 1 inch more in Rome.

A javelin thrower who competes near the equator would beat his northern record by a foot or more. If he were on a high plateau at the equator, he would have even a better record.

## Skier's fast turn

It is thrilling to see a skier swooping down a mountainside and making a sharp turn. How is this executed without excessive skidding?

In order to make a left turn he must receive a push toward that direction. He does this by bending his legs and feet to the left. This brings him up on the left edges of the skis. It allows him to push the snow to the right. You can see the snow fly in that direction.

He bends his body to the left to help him push to the right. The reaction of this push makes him go to the left.

## Changing seats in a small boat

Boating is a very popular sport. It can also be dangerous. One of the rules of safety you should try to obey is not to stand up or change seats in a small boat. Do you know why?

On page 77 you learned that an object is more stable when its center of gravity is low and near the center of the base. When you stand in a rowboat or a canoe you raise the center of gravity of the combination of you and the boat.

This lessens the stability. A slight shift of the boat, caused by wave action or by a sudden turn, may shift the center of gravity outside the base. The boat may capsize.

Try not to change seats away from a dock. But, if you must do it, stay *low* and hold on to the boat. Only one person at a time should change seats.

Try to distribute the rest of the boat's weight evenly by having the other occupants slide along their seats so that the boat remains balanced. Do not change while the boat is being rocked by waves or by the wake left by a passing boat.

# Index

# A CATALOG OF SELECTED
# DOVER BOOKS
## IN ALL FIELDS OF INTEREST

# A CATALOG OF SELECTED DOVER
# BOOKS IN ALL FIELDS OF INTEREST

DRAWINGS OF REMBRANDT, edited by Seymour Slive. Updated Lippmann, Hofstede de Groot edition, with definitive scholarly apparatus. All portraits, biblical sketches, landscapes, nudes. Oriental figures, classical studies, together with selection of work by followers. 550 illustrations. Total of 630pp. 9⅛ × 12¼.
21485-0, 21486-9 Pa., Two-vol. set $29.90

GHOST AND HORROR STORIES OF AMBROSE BIERCE, Ambrose Bierce. 24 tales vividly imagined, strangely prophetic, and decades ahead of their time in technical skill: "The Damned Thing," "An Inhabitant of Carcosa," "The Eyes of the Panther," "Moxon's Master," and 20 more. 199pp. 5⅜ × 8½. 20767-6 Pa. $4.95

ETHICAL WRITINGS OF MAIMONIDES, Maimonides. Most significant ethical works of great medieval sage, newly translated for utmost precision, readability. Laws Concerning Character Traits, Eight Chapters, more. 192pp. 5⅜ × 8½.
24522-5 Pa. $4.50

THE EXPLORATION OF THE COLORADO RIVER AND ITS CANYONS, J. W. Powell. Full text of Powell's 1,000-mile expedition down the fabled Colorado in 1869. Superb account of terrain, geology, vegetation, Indians, famine, mutiny, treacherous rapids, mighty canyons, during exploration of last unknown part of continental U.S. 400pp. 5⅜ × 8½. 20094-9 Pa. $7.95

HISTORY OF PHILOSOPHY, Julián Marías. Clearest one-volume history on the market. Every major philosopher and dozens of others, to Existentialism and later. 505pp. 5⅜ × 8½. 21739-6 Pa. $9.95

ALL ABOUT LIGHTNING, Martin A. Uman. Highly readable non-technical survey of nature and causes of lightning, thunderstorms, ball lightning, St. Elmo's Fire, much more. Illustrated. 192pp. 5⅜ × 8½. 25237-X Pa. $5.95

SAILING ALONE AROUND THE WORLD, Captain Joshua Slocum. First man to sail around the world, alone, in small boat. One of great feats of seamanship told in delightful manner. 67 illustrations. 294pp. 5⅜ × 8½. 20326-3 Pa. $4.95

LETTERS AND NOTES ON THE MANNERS, CUSTOMS AND CONDITIONS OF THE NORTH AMERICAN INDIANS, George Catlin. Classic account of life among Plains Indians: ceremonies, hunt, warfare, etc. 312 plates. 572pp. of text. 6⅛ × 9¼. 22118-0, 22119-9, Pa. Two-vol. set $17.90

ALASKA: The Harriman Expedition, 1899, John Burroughs, John Muir, et al. Informative, engrossing accounts of two-month, 9,000-mile expedition. Native peoples, wildlife, forests, geography, salmon industry, glaciers, more. Profusely illustrated. 240 black-and-white line drawings. 124 black-and-white photographs. 3 maps. Index. 576pp. 5⅜ × 8½. 25109-8 Pa. $11.95

THE BOOK OF BEASTS: Being a Translation from a Latin Bestiary of the Twelfth Century, T. H. White. Wonderful catalog real and fanciful beasts: manticore, griffin, phoenix, amphivius, jaculus, many more. White's witty erudite commentary on scientific, historical aspects. Fascinating glimpse of medieval mind. Illustrated. 296pp. 5⅜ × 8¼. (Available in U.S. only) 24609-4 Pa. $6.95

FRANK LLOYD WRIGHT: ARCHITECTURE AND NATURE With 160 Illustrations, Donald Hoffmann. Profusely illustrated study of influence of nature—especially prairie—on Wright's designs for Fallingwater, Robie House, Guggenheim Museum, other masterpieces. 96pp. 9¼ × 10¾. 25098-9 Pa. $8.95

FRANK LLOYD WRIGHT'S FALLINGWATER, Donald Hoffmann. Wright's famous waterfall house: planning and construction of organic idea. History of site, owners, Wright's personal involvement. Photographs of various stages of building. Preface by Edgar Kaufmann, Jr. 100 illustrations. 112pp. 9¼ × 10. 23671-4 Pa. $8.95

YEARS WITH FRANK LLOYD WRIGHT: Apprentice to Genius, Edgar Tafel. Insightful memoir by a former apprentice presents a revealing portrait of Wright the man, the inspired teacher, the greatest American architect. 372 black-and-white illustrations. Preface. Index. vi + 228pp. 8¼ × 11. 24801-1 Pa. $10.95

THE STORY OF KING ARTHUR AND HIS KNIGHTS, Howard Pyle. Enchanting version of King Arthur fable has delighted generations with imaginative narratives of exciting adventures and unforgettable illustrations by the author. 41 illustrations. xviii + 313pp. 6⅛ × 9¼. 21445-1 Pa. $6.95

THE GODS OF THE EGYPTIANS, E. A. Wallis Budge. Thorough coverage of numerous gods of ancient Egypt by foremost Egyptologist. Information on evolution of cults, rites and gods; the cult of Osiris; the Book of the Dead and its rites; the sacred animals and birds; Heaven and Hell; and more. 956pp. 6⅛ × 9¼. 22055-9, 22056-7 Pa., Two-vol. set $21.90

A THEOLOGICO-POLITICAL TREATISE, Benedict Spinoza. Also contains unfinished *Political Treatise*. Great classic on religious liberty, theory of government on common consent. R. Elwes translation. Total of 421pp. 5⅜ × 8½. 20249-6 Pa. $7.95

INCIDENTS OF TRAVEL IN CENTRAL AMERICA, CHIAPAS, AND YUCATAN, John L. Stephens. Almost single-handed discovery of Maya culture; exploration of ruined cities, monuments, temples; customs of Indians. 115 drawings. 892pp. 5⅜ × 8½. 22404-X, 22405-8 Pa., Two-vol. set $15.90

LOS CAPRICHOS, Francisco Goya. 80 plates of wild, grotesque monsters and caricatures. Prado manuscript included. 183pp. 6⅝ × 9⅝. 22384-1 Pa. $5.95

AUTOBIOGRAPHY: The Story of My Experiments with Truth, Mohandas K. Gandhi. Not hagiography, but Gandhi in his own words. Boyhood, legal studies, purification, the growth of the Satyagraha (nonviolent protest) movement. Critical, inspiring work of the man who freed India. 480pp. 5⅜ × 8½. (Available in U.S. only) 24593-4 Pa. $6.95

ILLUSTRATED DICTIONARY OF HISTORIC ARCHITECTURE, edited by Cyril M. Harris. Extraordinary compendium of clear, concise definitions for over 5,000 important architectural terms complemented by over 2,000 line drawings. Covers full spectrum of architecture from ancient ruins to 20th-century Modernism. Preface. 592pp. 7½ × 9⅝. 24444-X Pa. $15.95

THE NIGHT BEFORE CHRISTMAS, Clement Moore. Full text, and woodcuts from original 1848 book. Also critical, historical material. 19 illustrations. 40pp. 4⅝ × 6. 22797-9 Pa. $2.50

THE LESSON OF JAPANESE ARCHITECTURE: 165 Photographs, Jiro Harada. Memorable gallery of 165 photographs taken in the 1930's of exquisite Japanese homes of the well-to-do and historic buildings. 13 line diagrams. 192pp. 8⅜ × 11¼. 24778-3 Pa. $10.95

THE AUTOBIOGRAPHY OF CHARLES DARWIN AND SELECTED LETTERS, edited by Francis Darwin. The fascinating life of eccentric genius composed of an intimate memoir by Darwin (intended for his children); commentary by his son, Francis; hundreds of fragments from notebooks, journals, papers; and letters to and from Lyell, Hooker, Huxley, Wallace and Henslow. xi + 365pp. 5⅜ × 8. 20479-0 Pa. $6.95

WONDERS OF THE SKY: Observing Rainbows, Comets, Eclipses, the Stars and Other Phenomena, Fred Schaaf. Charming, easy-to-read poetic guide to all manner of celestial events visible to the naked eye. Mock suns, glories, Belt of Venus, more. Illustrated. 299pp. 5¼ × 8¼. 24402-4 Pa. $7.95

BURNHAM'S CELESTIAL HANDBOOK, Robert Burnham, Jr. Thorough guide to the stars beyond our solar system. Exhaustive treatment. Alphabetical by constellation: Andromeda to Cetus in Vol. 1; Chamaeleon to Orion in Vol. 2; and Pavo to Vulpecula in Vol. 3. Hundreds of illustrations. Index in Vol. 3. 2,000pp. 6⅛ × 9¼. 23567-X, 23568-8, 23673-0 Pa., Three-vol. set $41.85

STAR NAMES: Their Lore and Meaning, Richard Hinckley Allen. Fascinating history of names various cultures have given to constellations and literary and folkloristic uses that have been made of stars. Indexes to subjects. Arabic and Greek names. Biblical references. Bibliography. 563pp. 5⅜ × 8½. 21079-0 Pa. $8.95

THIRTY YEARS THAT SHOOK PHYSICS: The Story of Quantum Theory, George Gamow. Lucid, accessible introduction to influential theory of energy and matter. Careful explanations of Dirac's anti-particles, Bohr's model of the atom, much more. 12 plates. Numerous drawings. 240pp. 5⅜ × 8½. 24895-X Pa. $5.95

CHINESE DOMESTIC FURNITURE IN PHOTOGRAPHS AND MEASURED DRAWINGS, Gustav Ecke. A rare volume, now affordably priced for antique collectors, furniture buffs and art historians. Detailed review of styles ranging from early Shang to late Ming. Unabridged republication. 161 black-and-white drawings, photos. Total of 224pp. 8⅜ × 11¼. (Available in U.S. only) 25171-3 Pa. $13.95

VINCENT VAN GOGH: A Biography, Julius Meier-Graefe. Dynamic, penetrating study of artist's life, relationship with brother, Theo, painting techniques, travels, more. Readable, engrossing. 160pp. 5⅜ × 8½. (Available in U.S. only) 25253-1 Pa. $4.95

*CATALOG OF DOVER BOOKS*

HOW TO WRITE, Gertrude Stein. Gertrude Stein claimed anyone could understand her unconventional writing—here are clues to help. Fascinating improvisations, language experiments, explanations illuminate Stein's craft and the art of writing. Total of 414pp. 4⅝ × 6⅜. 23144-5 Pa. $6.95

ADVENTURES AT SEA IN THE GREAT AGE OF SAIL: Five Firsthand Narratives, edited by Elliot Snow. Rare true accounts of exploration, whaling, shipwreck, fierce natives, trade, shipboard life, more. 33 illustrations. Introduction. 353pp. 5⅜ × 8½. 25177-2 Pa. $8.95

THE HERBAL OR GENERAL HISTORY OF PLANTS, John Gerard. Classic descriptions of about 2,850 plants—with over 2,700 illustrations—includes Latin and English names, physical descriptions, varieties, time and place of growth, more. 2,706 illustrations. xlv + 1,678pp. 8½ × 12¼. 23147-X Cloth. $75.00

DOROTHY AND THE WIZARD IN OZ, L. Frank Baum. Dorothy and the Wizard visit the center of the Earth, where people are vegetables, glass houses grow and Oz characters reappear. Classic sequel to *Wizard of Oz*. 256pp. 5⅜ × 8.
24714-7 Pa. $5.95

SONGS OF EXPERIENCE: Facsimile Reproduction with 26 Plates in Full Color, William Blake. This facsimile of Blake's original "Illuminated Book" reproduces 26 full-color plates from a rare 1826 edition. Includes "The Tyger," "London," "Holy Thursday," and other immortal poems. 26 color plates. Printed text of poems. 48pp. 5¼ × 7. 24636-1 Pa. $3.95

SONGS OF INNOCENCE, William Blake. The first and most popular of Blake's famous "Illuminated Books," in a facsimile edition reproducing all 31 brightly colored plates. Additional printed text of each poem. 64pp. 5¼ × 7.
22764-2 Pa. $3.95

PRECIOUS STONES, Max Bauer. Classic, thorough study of diamonds, rubies, emeralds, garnets, etc.: physical character, occurrence, properties, use, similar topics. 20 plates, 8 in color. 94 figures. 659pp. 6⅛ × 9¼.
21910-0, 21911-9 Pa., Two-vol. set $15.90

ENCYCLOPEDIA OF VICTORIAN NEEDLEWORK, S. F. A. Caulfeild and Blanche Saward. Full, precise descriptions of stitches, techniques for dozens of needlecrafts—most exhaustive reference of its kind. Over 800 figures. Total of 679pp. 8⅛ × 11. Two volumes. Vol. 1 22800-2 Pa. $11.95
Vol. 2 22801-0 Pa. $11.95

THE MARVELOUS LAND OF OZ, L. Frank Baum. Second Oz book, the Scarecrow and Tin Woodman are back with hero named Tip, Oz magic. 136 illustrations. 287pp. 5⅜ × 8½. 20692-0 Pa. $5.95

WILD FOWL DECOYS, Joel Barber. Basic book on the subject, by foremost authority and collector. Reveals history of decoy making and rigging, place in American culture, different kinds of decoys, how to make them, and how to use them. 140 plates. 156pp. 7⅞ × 10¾. 20011-6 Pa. $8.95

HISTORY OF LACE, Mrs. Bury Palliser. Definitive, profusely illustrated chronicle of lace from earliest times to late 19th century. Laces of Italy, Greece, England, France, Belgium, etc. Landmark of needlework scholarship. 266 illustrations. 672pp. 6⅛ × 9¼. 24742-2 Pa. $14.95

ILLUSTRATED GUIDE TO SHAKER FURNITURE, Robert Meader. All furniture and appurtenances, with much on unknown local styles. 235 photos. 146pp. 9 × 12. 22819-3 Pa. $8.95

WHALE SHIPS AND WHALING: A Pictorial Survey, George Francis Dow. Over 200 vintage engravings, drawings, photographs of barks, brigs, cutters, other vessels. Also harpoons, lances, whaling guns, many other artifacts. Comprehensive text by foremost authority. 207 black-and-white illustrations. 288pp. 6 × 9. 24808-9 Pa. $9.95

THE BERTRAMS, Anthony Trollope. Powerful portrayal of blind self-will and thwarted ambition includes one of Trollope's most heartrending love stories. 497pp. 5⅜ × 8½. 25119-5 Pa. $9.95

ADVENTURES WITH A HAND LENS, Richard Headstrom. Clearly written guide to observing and studying flowers and grasses, fish scales, moth and insect wings, egg cases, buds, feathers, seeds, leaf scars, moss, molds, ferns, common crystals, etc.—all with an ordinary, inexpensive magnifying glass. 209 exact line drawings aid in your discoveries. 220pp. 5⅜ × 8½. 23330-8 Pa. $4.95

RODIN ON ART AND ARTISTS, Auguste Rodin. Great sculptor's candid, wide-ranging comments on meaning of art; great artists; relation of sculpture to poetry, painting, music; philosophy of life, more. 76 superb black-and-white illustrations of Rodin's sculpture, drawings and prints. 119pp. 8⅜ × 11¼. 24487-3 Pa. $7.95

FIFTY CLASSIC FRENCH FILMS, 1912–1982: A Pictorial Record, Anthony Slide. Memorable stills from Grand Illusion, Beauty and the Beast, Hiroshima, Mon Amour, many more. Credits, plot synopses, reviews, etc. 160pp. 8¼ × 11. 25256-6 Pa. $11.95

THE PRINCIPLES OF PSYCHOLOGY, William James. Famous long course complete, unabridged. Stream of thought, time perception, memory, experimental methods; great work decades ahead of its time. 94 figures. 1,391pp. 5⅜ × 8½. 20381-6, 20382-4 Pa., Two-vol. set $23.90

BODIES IN A BOOKSHOP, R. T. Campbell. Challenging mystery of blackmail and murder with ingenious plot and superbly drawn characters. In the best tradition of British suspense fiction. 192pp. 5⅜ × 8½. 24720-1 Pa. $4.95

CALLAS: PORTRAIT OF A PRIMA DONNA, George Jellinek. Renowned commentator on the musical scene chronicles incredible career and life of the most controversial, fascinating, influential operatic personality of our time. 64 black-and-white photographs. 416pp. 5⅜ × 8¼. 25047-4 Pa. $8.95

GEOMETRY, RELATIVITY AND THE FOURTH DIMENSION, Rudolph Rucker. Exposition of fourth dimension, concepts of relativity as Flatland characters continue adventures. Popular, easily followed yet accurate, profound. 141 illustrations. 133pp. 5⅜ × 8½. 23400-2 Pa. $4.95

HOUSEHOLD STORIES BY THE BROTHERS GRIMM, with pictures by Walter Crane. 53 classic stories—Rumpelstiltskin, Rapunzel, Hansel and Gretel, the Fisherman and his Wife, Snow White, Tom Thumb, Sleeping Beauty, Cinderella, and so much more—lavishly illustrated with original 19th century drawings. 114 illustrations. x + 269pp. 5⅜ × 8½. 21080-4 Pa. $4.95

SUNDIALS, Albert Waugh. Far and away the best, most thorough coverage of ideas, mathematics concerned, types, construction, adjusting anywhere. Over 100 illustrations. 230pp. 5⅜ × 8½. 22947-5 Pa. $5.95

PICTURE HISTORY OF THE NORMANDIE: With 190 Illustrations, Frank O. Braynard. Full story of legendary French ocean liner: Art Deco interiors, design innovations, furnishings, celebrities, maiden voyage, tragic fire, much more. Extensive text. 144pp. 8⅞ × 11¾. 25257-4 Pa. $10.95

THE FIRST AMERICAN COOKBOOK: A Facsimile of "American Cookery," 1796, Amelia Simmons. Facsimile of the first American-written cookbook published in the United States contains authentic recipes for colonial favorites—pumpkin pudding, winter squash pudding, spruce beer, Indian slapjacks, and more. Introductory Essay and Glossary of colonial cooking terms. 80pp. 5⅜ × 8½.
24710-4 Pa. $3.50

101 PUZZLES IN THOUGHT AND LOGIC, C. R. Wylie, Jr. Solve murders and robberies, find out which fishermen are liars, how a blind man could possibly identify a color—purely by your own reasoning! 107pp. 5⅜ × 8½. 20367-0 Pa. $2.50

ANCIENT EGYPTIAN MYTHS AND LEGENDS, Lewis Spence. Examines animism, totemism, fetishism, creation myths, deities, alchemy, art and magic, other topics. Over 50 illustrations. 432pp. 5⅜ × 8½. 26525-0 Pa. $8.95

ANTHROPOLOGY AND MODERN LIFE, Franz Boas. Great anthropologist's classic treatise on race and culture. Introduction by Ruth Bunzel. Only inexpensive paperback edition. 255pp. 5⅜ × 8½. 25245-0 Pa. $6.95

THE TALE OF PETER RABBIT, Beatrix Potter. The inimitable Peter's terrifying adventure in Mr. McGregor's garden, with all 27 wonderful, full-color Potter illustrations. 55pp. 4¼ × 5½. (Available in U.S. only) 22827-4 Pa. $1.75

THREE PROPHETIC SCIENCE FICTION NOVELS, H. G. Wells. *When the Sleeper Wakes, A Story of the Days to Come* and *The Time Machine* (full version). 335pp. 5⅜ × 8½. (Available in U.S. only) 20605-X Pa. $6.95

APICIUS COOKERY AND DINING IN IMPERIAL ROME, edited and translated by Joseph Dommers Vehling. Oldest known cookbook in existence offers readers a clear picture of what foods Romans ate, how they prepared them, etc. 49 illustrations. 301pp. 6⅛ × 9¼. 23563-7 Pa. $7.95

SHAKESPEARE LEXICON AND QUOTATION DICTIONARY, Alexander Schmidt. Full definitions, locations, shades of meaning of every word in plays and poems. More than 50,000 exact quotations. 1,485pp. 6½ × 9¼.
22726-X, 22727-8 Pa., Two-vol. set $31.90

THE WORLD'S GREAT SPEECHES, edited by Lewis Copeland and Lawrence W. Lamm. Vast collection of 278 speeches from Greeks to 1970. Powerful and effective models; unique look at history. 842pp. 5⅜ × 8½. 20468-5 Pa. $12.95

THE BLUE FAIRY BOOK, Andrew Lang. The first, most famous collection, with many familiar tales: Little Red Riding Hood, Aladdin and the Wonderful Lamp, Puss in Boots, Sleeping Beauty, Hansel and Gretel, Rumpelstiltskin; 37 in all. 138 illustrations. 390pp. 5⅜ × 8½. 21437-0 Pa. $6.95

THE STORY OF THE CHAMPIONS OF THE ROUND TABLE, Howard Pyle. Sir Launcelot, Sir Tristram and Sir Percival in spirited adventures of love and triumph retold in Pyle's inimitable style. 50 drawings, 31 full-page. xviii + 329pp. 6½ × 9¼. 21883-X Pa. $7.95

THE MYTHS OF THE NORTH AMERICAN INDIANS, Lewis Spence. Myths and legends of the Algonquins, Iroquois, Pawnees and Sioux with comprehensive historical and ethnological commentary. 36 illustrations. 5⅜ × 8½. 25967-6 Pa. $8.95

GREAT DINOSAUR HUNTERS AND THEIR DISCOVERIES, Edwin H. Colbert. Fascinating, lavishly illustrated chronicle of dinosaur research, 1820's to 1960. Achievements of Cope, Marsh, Brown, Buckland, Mantell, Huxley, many others. 384pp. 5¼ × 8¼. 24701-5 Pa. $7.95

THE TASTEMAKERS, Russell Lynes. Informal, illustrated social history of American taste 1850's–1950's. First popularized categories Highbrow, Lowbrow, Middlebrow. 129 illustrations. New (1979) afterword. 384pp. 6 × 9. 23993-4 Pa. $8.95

DOUBLE CROSS PURPOSES, Ronald A. Knox. A treasure hunt in the Scottish Highlands, an old map, unidentified corpse, surprise discoveries keep reader guessing in this cleverly intricate tale of financial skullduggery. 2 black-and-white maps. 320pp. 5⅜ × 8½. (Available in U.S. only) 25032-6 Pa. $6.95

AUTHENTIC VICTORIAN DECORATION AND ORNAMENTATION IN FULL COLOR: 46 Plates from "Studies in Design," Christopher Dresser. Superb full-color lithographs reproduced from rare original portfolio of a major Victorian designer. 48pp. 9¼ × 12¼. 25083-0 Pa. $7.95

PRIMITIVE ART, Franz Boas. Remains the best text ever prepared on subject, thoroughly discussing Indian, African, Asian, Australian, and, especially, Northern American primitive art. Over 950 illustrations show ceramics, masks, totem poles, weapons, textiles, paintings, much more. 376pp. 5⅜ × 8. 20025-6 Pa. $7.95

SIDELIGHTS ON RELATIVITY, Albert Einstein. Unabridged republication of two lectures delivered by the great physicist in 1920–21. *Ether and Relativity* and *Geometry and Experience*. Elegant ideas in non-mathematical form, accessible to intelligent layman. vi + 56pp. 5⅜ × 8½. 24511-X Pa. $2.95

THE WIT AND HUMOR OF OSCAR WILDE, edited by Alvin Redman. More than 1,000 ripostes, paradoxes, wisecracks: Work is the curse of the drinking classes, I can resist everything except temptation, etc. 258pp. 5⅜ × 8½. 20602-5 Pa. $4.95

ADVENTURES WITH A MICROSCOPE, Richard Headstrom. 59 adventures with clothing fibers, protozoa, ferns and lichens, roots and leaves, much more. 142 illustrations. 232pp. 5⅜ × 8½. 23471-1 Pa. $3.95

PLANTS OF THE BIBLE, Harold N. Moldenke and Alma L. Moldenke. Standard reference to all 230 plants mentioned in Scriptures. Latin name, biblical reference, uses, modern identity, much more. Unsurpassed encyclopedic resource for scholars, botanists, nature lovers, students of Bible. Bibliography. Indexes. 123 black-and-white illustrations. 384pp. 6 × 9.  25069-5 Pa. $8.95

FAMOUS AMERICAN WOMEN: A Biographical Dictionary from Colonial Times to the Present, Robert McHenry, ed. From Pocahontas to Rosa Parks, 1,035 distinguished American women documented in separate biographical entries. Accurate, up-to-date data, numerous categories, spans 400 years. Indices. 493pp. 6½ × 9¼.  24523-3 Pa. $10.95

THE FABULOUS INTERIORS OF THE GREAT OCEAN LINERS IN HISTORIC PHOTOGRAPHS, William H. Miller, Jr. Some 200 superb photographs capture exquisite interiors of world's great "floating palaces"—1890's to 1980's: *Titanic, Ile de France, Queen Elizabeth, United States, Europa*, more. Approx. 200 black-and-white photographs. Captions. Text. Introduction. 160pp. 8⅜ × 11¼.
24756-2 Pa. $9.95

THE GREAT LUXURY LINERS, 1927-1954: A Photographic Record, William H. Miller, Jr. Nostalgic tribute to heyday of ocean liners. 186 photos of Ile de France, Normandie, Leviathan, Queen Elizabeth, United States, many others. Interior and exterior views. Introduction. Captions. 160pp. 9 × 12.
24056-8 Pa. $10.95

A NATURAL HISTORY OF THE DUCKS, John Charles Phillips. Great landmark of ornithology offers complete detailed coverage of nearly 200 species and subspecies of ducks: gadwall, sheldrake, merganser, pintail, many more. 74 full-color plates, 102 black-and-white. Bibliography. Total of 1,920pp. 8⅜ × 11¼.
25141-1, 25142-X Cloth. Two-vol. set $100.00

THE SEAWEED HANDBOOK: An Illustrated Guide to Seaweeds from North Carolina to Canada, Thomas F. Lee. Concise reference covers 78 species. Scientific and common names, habitat, distribution, more. Finding keys for easy identification. 224pp. 5⅜ × 8½.  25215-9 Pa. $6.95

THE TEN BOOKS OF ARCHITECTURE: The 1755 Leoni Edition, Leon Battista Alberti. Rare classic helped introduce the glories of ancient architecture to the Renaissance. 68 black-and-white plates. 336pp. 8⅜ × 11¼.  25239-6 Pa. $14.95

MISS MACKENZIE, Anthony Trollope. Minor masterpieces by Victorian master unmasks many truths about life in 19th-century England. First inexpensive edition in years. 392pp. 5⅜ × 8½.  25201-9 Pa. $8.95

THE RIME OF THE ANCIENT MARINER, Gustave Doré, Samuel Taylor Coleridge. Dramatic engravings considered by many to be his greatest work. The terrifying space of the open sea, the storms and whirlpools of an unknown ocean, the ice of Antarctica, more—all rendered in a powerful, chilling manner. Full text. 38 plates. 77pp. 9¼ × 12.  22305-1 Pa. $4.95

THE EXPEDITIONS OF ZEBULON MONTGOMERY PIKE, Zebulon Montgomery Pike. Fascinating first-hand accounts (1805-6) of exploration of Mississippi River, Indian wars, capture by Spanish dragoons, much more. 1,088pp. 5⅜ × 8½.  25254-X, 25255-8 Pa. Two-vol. set $25.90

A CONCISE HISTORY OF PHOTOGRAPHY: Third Revised Edition, Helmut Gernsheim. Best one-volume history—camera obscura, photochemistry, daguerreotypes, evolution of cameras, film, more. Also artistic aspects—landscape, portraits, fine art, etc. 281 black-and-white photographs. 26 in color. 176pp. 8⅜ × 11¼. 25128-4 Pa. $13.95

THE DORÉ BIBLE ILLUSTRATIONS, Gustave Doré. 241 detailed plates from the Bible: the Creation scenes, Adam and Eve, Flood, Babylon, battle sequences, life of Jesus, etc. Each plate is accompanied by the verses from the King James version of the Bible. 241pp. 9 × 12. 23004-X Pa. $9.95

WANDERINGS IN WEST AFRICA, Richard F. Burton. Great Victorian scholar/adventurer's invaluable descriptions of African tribal rituals, fetishism, culture, art, much more. Fascinating 19th-century account. 624pp. 5⅜ × 8½. 26890-X Pa. $12.95

FLATLAND, E. A. Abbott. Intriguing and enormously popular science-fiction classic explores the complexities of trying to survive as a two-dimensional being in a three-dimensional world. Amusingly illustrated by the author. 16 illustrations. 103pp. 5⅜ × 8½. 20001-9 Pa. $2.50

THE HISTORY OF THE LEWIS AND CLARK EXPEDITION, Meriwether Lewis and William Clark, edited by Elliott Coues. Classic edition of Lewis and Clark's day-by-day journals that later became the basis for U.S. claims to Oregon and the West. Accurate and invaluable geographical, botanical, biological, meteorological and anthropological material. Total of 1,508pp. 5⅜ × 8½.
21268-8, 21269-6, 21270-X Pa. Three-vol. set $26.85

LANGUAGE, TRUTH AND LOGIC, Alfred J. Ayer. Famous, clear introduction to Vienna, Cambridge schools of Logical Positivism. Role of philosophy, elimination of metaphysics, nature of analysis, etc. 160pp. 5⅜ × 8½. (Available in U.S. and Canada only) 20010-8 Pa. $3.95

MATHEMATICS FOR THE NONMATHEMATICIAN, Morris Kline. Detailed, college-level treatment of mathematics in cultural and historical context, with numerous exercises. For liberal arts students. Preface. Recommended Reading Lists. Tables. Index. Numerous black-and-white figures. xvi + 641pp. 5⅜ × 8½.
24823-2 Pa. $11.95

HANDBOOK OF PICTORIAL SYMBOLS, Rudolph Modley. 3,250 signs and symbols, many systems in full; official or heavy commercial use. Arranged by subject. Most in Pictorial Archive series. 143pp. 8⅛ × 11. 23357-X Pa. $6.95

INCIDENTS OF TRAVEL IN YUCATAN, John L. Stephens. Classic (1843) exploration of jungles of Yucatan, looking for evidences of Maya civilization. Travel adventures, Mexican and Indian culture, etc. Total of 669pp. 5⅜ × 8½.
20926-1, 20927-X Pa., Two-vol. set $11.90

DEGAS: An Intimate Portrait, Ambroise Vollard. Charming, anecdotal memoir by famous art dealer of one of the greatest 19th-century French painters. 14 black-and-white illustrations. Introduction by Harold L. Van Doren. 96pp. 5⅜ × 8½.
25131-4 Pa. $4.95

PERSONAL NARRATIVE OF A PILGRIMAGE TO ALMANDINAH AND MECCAH, Richard Burton. Great travel classic by remarkably colorful personality. Burton, disguised as a Moroccan, visited sacred shrines of Islam, narrowly escaping death. 47 illustrations. 959pp. 5⅜ × 8½. 21217-3, 21218-1 Pa., Two-vol. set $19.90

PHRASE AND WORD ORIGINS, A. H. Holt. Entertaining, reliable, modern study of more than 1,200 colorful words, phrases, origins and histories. Much unexpected information. 254pp. 5⅜ × 8½. 20758-7 Pa. $5.95

THE RED THUMB MARK, R. Austin Freeman. In this first Dr. Thorndyke case, the great scientific detective draws fascinating conclusions from the nature of a single fingerprint. Exciting story, authentic science. 320pp. 5⅜ × 8½. (Available in U.S. only) 25210-8 Pa. $6.95

AN EGYPTIAN HIEROGLYPHIC DICTIONARY, E. A. Wallis Budge. Monumental work containing about 25,000 words or terms that occur in texts ranging from 3000 B.C. to 600 A.D. Each entry consists of a transliteration of the word, the word in hieroglyphs, and the meaning in English. 1,314pp. 6⅜ × 10.
23615-3, 23616-1 Pa., Two-vol. set $35.90

THE COMPLEAT STRATEGYST: Being a Primer on the Theory of Games of Strategy, J. D. Williams. Highly entertaining classic describes, with many illustrated examples, how to select best strategies in conflict situations. Prefaces. Appendices. xvi + 268pp. 5⅜ × 8½. 25101-2 Pa. $6.95

THE ROAD TO OZ, L. Frank Baum. Dorothy meets the Shaggy Man, little Button-Bright and the Rainbow's beautiful daughter in this delightful trip to the magical Land of Oz. 272pp. 5⅜ × 8. 25208-6 Pa. $5.95

POINT AND LINE TO PLANE, Wassily Kandinsky. Seminal exposition of role of point, line, other elements in non-objective painting. Essential to understanding 20th-century art. 127 illustrations. 192pp. 6½ × 9¼. 23808-3 Pa. $5.95

LADY ANNA, Anthony Trollope. Moving chronicle of Countess Lovel's bitter struggle to win for herself and daughter Anna their rightful rank and fortune—perhaps at cost of sanity itself. 384pp. 5⅜ × 8½. 24669-8 Pa. $8.95

EGYPTIAN MAGIC, E. A. Wallis Budge. Sums up all that is known about magic in Ancient Egypt: the role of magic in controlling the gods, powerful amulets that warded off evil spirits, scarabs of immortality, use of wax images, formulas and spells, the secret name, much more. 253pp. 5⅜ × 8½. 22681-6 Pa. $4.50

THE DANCE OF SIVA, Ananda Coomaraswamy. Preeminent authority unfolds the vast metaphysic of India: the revelation of her art, conception of the universe, social organization, etc. 27 reproductions of art masterpieces. 192pp. 5⅜ × 8½.
24817-8 Pa. $5.95

CHRISTMAS CUSTOMS AND TRADITIONS, Clement A. Miles. Origin, evolution, significance of religious, secular practices. Caroling, gifts, yule logs, much more. Full, scholarly yet fascinating; non-sectarian. 400pp. 5⅜ × 8½.
23354-5 Pa. $6.95

THE HUMAN FIGURE IN MOTION, Eadweard Muybridge. More than 4,500 stopped-action photos, in action series, showing undraped men, women, children jumping, lying down, throwing, sitting, wrestling, carrying, etc. 390pp. 7⅞ × 10⅝.
20204-6 Cloth. $24.95

THE MAN WHO WAS THURSDAY, Gilbert Keith Chesterton. Witty, fast-paced novel about a club of anarchists in turn-of-the-century London. Brilliant social, religious, philosophical speculations. 128pp. 5⅜ × 8½. 25121-7 Pa. $3.95

A CEZANNE SKETCHBOOK: Figures, Portraits, Landscapes and Still Lifes, Paul Cezanne. Great artist experiments with tonal effects, light, mass, other qualities in over 100 drawings. A revealing view of developing master painter, precursor of Cubism. 102 black-and-white illustrations. 144pp. 8¾ × 6⅜. 24790-2 Pa. $6.95

AN ENCYCLOPEDIA OF BATTLES: Accounts of Over 1,560 Battles from 1479 B.C. to the Present, David Eggenberger. Presents essential details of every major battle in recorded history, from the first battle of Megiddo in 1479 B.C. to Grenada in 1984. List of Battle Maps. New Appendix covering the years 1967–1984. Index. 99 illustrations. 544pp. 6½ × 9¼. 24913-1 Pa. $14.95

AN ETYMOLOGICAL DICTIONARY OF MODERN ENGLISH, Ernest Weekley. Richest, fullest work, by foremost British lexicographer. Detailed word histories. Inexhaustible. Total of 856pp. 6½ × 9¼.
21873-2, 21874-0 Pa., Two-vol. set $19.90

WEBSTER'S AMERICAN MILITARY BIOGRAPHIES, edited by Robert McHenry. Over 1,000 figures who shaped 3 centuries of American military history. Detailed biographies of Nathan Hale, Douglas MacArthur, Mary Hallaren, others. Chronologies of engagements, more. Introduction. Addenda. 1,033 entries in alphabetical order. xi + 548pp. 6½ × 9¼. (Available in U.S. only)
24758-9 Pa. $13.95

LIFE IN ANCIENT EGYPT, Adolf Erman. Detailed older account, with much not in more recent books: domestic life, religion, magic, medicine, commerce, and whatever else needed for complete picture. Many illustrations. 597pp. 5⅜ × 8½.
22632-8 Pa. $8.95

HISTORIC COSTUME IN PICTURES, Braun & Schneider. Over 1,450 costumed figures shown, covering a wide variety of peoples: kings, emperors, nobles, priests, servants, soldiers, scholars, townsfolk, peasants, merchants, courtiers, cavaliers, and more. 256pp. 8⅜ × 11¼. 23150-X Pa. $9.95

THE NOTEBOOKS OF LEONARDO DA VINCI, edited by J. P. Richter. Extracts from manuscripts reveal great genius; on painting, sculpture, anatomy, sciences, geography, etc. Both Italian and English. 186 ms. pages reproduced, plus 500 additional drawings, including studies for *Last Supper, Sforza* monument, etc. 860pp. 7⅞ × 10¾. (Available in U.S. only) 22572-0, 22573-9 Pa., Two-vol. set $31.90

THE ART NOUVEAU STYLE BOOK OF ALPHONSE MUCHA: All 72 Plates from "Documents Decoratifs" in Original Color, Alphonse Mucha. Rare copyright-free design portfolio by high priest of Art Nouveau. Jewelry, wallpaper, stained glass, furniture, figure studies, plant and animal motifs, etc. Only complete one-volume edition. 80pp. 9⅜ × 12¼. 24044-4 Pa. $9.95

ANIMALS: 1,419 COPYRIGHT-FREE ILLUSTRATIONS OF MAMMALS, BIRDS, FISH, INSECTS, ETC., edited by Jim Harter. Clear wood engravings present, in extremely lifelike poses, over 1,000 species of animals. One of the most extensive pictorial sourcebooks of its kind. Captions. Index. 284pp. 9 × 12. 23766-4 Pa. $9.95

OBELISTS FLY HIGH, C. Daly King. Masterpiece of American detective fiction, long out of print, involves murder on a 1935 transcontinental flight—"a very thrilling story"—NY Times. Unabridged and unaltered republication of the edition published by William Collins Sons & Co. Ltd., London, 1935. 288pp. 5⅜ × 8½. (Available in U.S. only) 25036-9 Pa. $5.95

VICTORIAN AND EDWARDIAN FASHION: A Photographic Survey, Alison Gernsheim. First fashion history completely illustrated by contemporary photographs. Full text plus 235 photos, 1840–1914, in which many celebrities appear. 240pp. 6½ × 9¼. 24205-6 Pa. $8.95

THE ART OF THE FRENCH ILLUSTRATED BOOK, 1700–1914, Gordon N. Ray. Over 630 superb book illustrations by Fragonard, Delacroix, Daumier, Doré, Grandville, Manet, Mucha, Steinlen, Toulouse-Lautrec and many others. Preface. Introduction. 633 halftones. Indices of artists, authors & titles, binders and provenances. Appendices. Bibliography. 608pp. 8⅜ × 11¼. 25086-5 Pa. $24.95

THE WONDERFUL WIZARD OF OZ, L. Frank Baum. Facsimile in full color of America's finest children's classic. 143 illustrations by W. W. Denslow. 267pp. 5⅜ × 8½. 20691-2 Pa. $7.95

FOLLOWING THE EQUATOR: A Journey Around the World, Mark Twain. Great writer's 1897 account of circumnavigating the globe by steamship. Ironic humor, keen observations, vivid and fascinating descriptions of exotic places. 197 illustrations. 720pp. 5⅜ × 8½. 26113-1 Pa. $15.95

THE FRIENDLY STARS, Martha Evans Martin & Donald Howard Menzel. Classic text marshalls the stars together in an engaging, non-technical survey, presenting them as sources of beauty in night sky. 23 illustrations. Foreword. 2 star charts. Index. 147pp. 5⅜ × 8½. 21099-5 Pa. $3.95

FADS AND FALLACIES IN THE NAME OF SCIENCE, Martin Gardner. Fair, witty appraisal of cranks, quacks, and quackeries of science and pseudoscience: hollow earth, Velikovsky, orgone energy, Dianetics, flying saucers, Bridey Murphy, food and medical fads, etc. Revised, expanded In the Name of Science. "A very able and even-tempered presentation."—The New Yorker. 363pp. 5⅜ × 8. 20394-8 Pa. $6.95

ANCIENT EGYPT: ITS CULTURE AND HISTORY, J. E Manchip White. From pre-dynastics through Ptolemies: society, history, political structure, religion, daily life, literature, cultural heritage. 48 plates. 217pp. 5⅜ × 8½. 22548-8 Pa. $5.95

SIR HARRY HOTSPUR OF HUMBLETHWAITE, Anthony Trollope. Incisive, unconventional psychological study of a conflict between a wealthy baronet, his idealistic daughter, and their scapegrace cousin. The 1870 novel in its first inexpensive edition in years. 250pp. 5⅜ × 8½. 24953-0 Pa. $6.95

LASERS AND HOLOGRAPHY, Winston E. Kock. Sound introduction to burgeoning field, expanded (1981) for second edition. Wave patterns, coherence, lasers, diffraction, zone plates, properties of holograms, recent advances. 84 illustrations. 160pp. 5⅜ × 8¼. (Except in United Kingdom) 24041-X Pa. $3.95

INTRODUCTION TO ARTIFICIAL INTELLIGENCE: SECOND, EN-LARGED EDITION, Philip C. Jackson, Jr. Comprehensive survey of artificial intelligence—the study of how machines (computers) can be made to act intelligently. Includes introductory and advanced material. Extensive notes updating the main text. 132 black-and-white illustrations. 512pp. 5⅜ × 8½. 24864-X Pa. $8.95

HISTORY OF INDIAN AND INDONESIAN ART, Ananda K. Coomaraswamy. Over 400 illustrations illuminate classic study of Indian art from earliest Harappa finds to early 20th century. Provides philosophical, religious and social insights. 304pp. 6⅜ × 9⅜. 25005-9 Pa. $11.95

THE GOLEM, Gustav Meyrink. Most famous supernatural novel in modern European literature, set in Ghetto of Old Prague around 1890. Compelling story of mystical experiences, strange transformations, profound terror. 13 black-and-white illustrations. 224pp. 5⅜ × 8½. (Available in U.S. only) 25025-3 Pa. $6.95

PICTORIAL ENCYCLOPEDIA OF HISTORIC ARCHITECTURAL PLANS, DETAILS AND ELEMENTS: With 1,880 Line Drawings of Arches, Domes, Doorways, Facades, Gables, Windows, etc., John Theodore Haneman. Sourcebook of inspiration for architects, designers, others. Bibliography. Captions. 141pp. 9 × 12. 24605-1 Pa. $7.95

BENCHLEY LOST AND FOUND, Robert Benchley. Finest humor from early 30's, about pet peeves, child psychologists, post office and others. Mostly unavailable elsewhere. 73 illustrations by Peter Arno and others. 183pp. 5⅜ × 8½. 22410-4 Pa. $4.95

ERTÉ GRAPHICS, Erté. Collection of striking color graphics: Seasons, Alphabet, Numerals, Aces and Precious Stones. 50 plates, including 4 on covers. 48pp. 9⅜ × 12¼. 23580-7 Pa. $7.95

THE JOURNAL OF HENRY D. THOREAU, edited by Bradford Torrey, F. H. Allen. Complete reprinting of 14 volumes, 1837-61, over two million words; the sourcebooks for Walden, etc. Definitive. All original sketches, plus 75 photographs. 1,804pp. 8½ × 12¼. 20312-3, 20313-1 Cloth., Two-vol. set $125.00

CASTLES: THEIR CONSTRUCTION AND HISTORY, Sidney Toy. Traces castle development from ancient roots. Nearly 200 photographs and drawings illustrate moats, keeps, baileys, many other features. Caernarvon, Dover Castles, Hadrian's Wall, Tower of London, dozens more. 256pp. 5⅜ × 8¼. 24898-4 Pa. $6.95

# CATALOG OF DOVER BOOKS

AMERICAN CLIPPER SHIPS: 1833–1858, Octavius T. Howe & Frederick C. Matthews. Fully-illustrated, encyclopedic review of 352 clipper ships from the period of America's greatest maritime supremacy. Introduction. 109 halftones. 5 black-and-white line illustrations. Index. Total of 928pp. 5⅜ × 8½.
25115-2, 25116-0 Pa., Two-vol. set $17.90

TOWARDS A NEW ARCHITECTURE, Le Corbusier. Pioneering manifesto by great architect, near legendary founder of "International School." Technical and aesthetic theories, views on industry, economics, relation of form to function, "mass-production spirit," much more. Profusely illustrated. Unabridged translation of 13th French edition. Introduction by Frederick Etchells. 320pp. 6⅛ × 9¼. (Available in U.S. only)
25023-7 Pa. $8.95

THE BOOK OF KELLS, edited by Blanche Cirker. Inexpensive collection of 32 full-color, full-page plates from the greatest illuminated manuscript of the Middle Ages, painstakingly reproduced from rare facsimile edition. Publisher's Note. Captions. 32pp. 9⅜ × 12¼.
24345-1 Pa. $4.95

BEST SCIENCE FICTION STORIES OF H. G. WELLS, H. G. Wells. Full novel *The Invisible Man*, plus 17 short stories: "The Crystal Egg," "Aepyornis Island," "The Strange Orchid," etc. 303pp. 5⅜ × 8½. (Available in U.S. only)
21531-8 Pa. $6.95

AMERICAN SAILING SHIPS: Their Plans and History, Charles G. Davis. Photos, construction details of schooners, frigates, clippers, other sailcraft of 18th to early 20th centuries—plus entertaining discourse on design, rigging, nautical lore, much more. 137 black-and-white illustrations. 240pp. 6⅛ × 9¼.
24658-2 Pa. $6.95

ENTERTAINING MATHEMATICAL PUZZLES, Martin Gardner. Selection of author's favorite conundrums involving arithmetic, money, speed, etc., with lively commentary. Complete solutions. 112pp. 5⅜ × 8½.
25211-6 Pa. $2.95

THE WILL TO BELIEVE, HUMAN IMMORTALITY, William James. Two books bound together. Effect of irrational on logical, and arguments for human immortality. 402pp. 5⅜ × 8½.
20291-7 Pa. $7.95

THE HAUNTED MONASTERY and THE CHINESE MAZE MURDERS, Robert Van Gulik. 2 full novels by Van Gulik continue adventures of Judge Dee and his companions. An evil Taoist monastery, seemingly supernatural events; overgrown topiary maze that hides strange crimes. Set in 7th-century China. 27 illustrations. 328pp. 5⅜ × 8½.
23502-5 Pa. $6.95

CELEBRATED CASES OF JUDGE DEE (DEE GOONG AN), translated by Robert Van Gulik. Authentic 18th-century Chinese detective novel; Dee and associates solve three interlocked cases. Led to Van Gulik's own stories with same characters. Extensive introduction. 9 illustrations. 237pp. 5⅜ × 8½.
23337-5 Pa. $5.95

*Prices subject to change without notice.*
Available at your book dealer or write for free catalog to Dept. GI, Dover Publications, Inc., 31 East 2nd St., Mineola, N.Y. 11501. Dover publishes more than 175 books each year on science, elementary and advanced mathematics, biology, music, art, literary history, social sciences and other areas.